Ephesians
and All that Jazz

Ephesians and All that Jazz

Riffing with Paul: A Transliteration

TOM ANDERSON

foreword by William Jeynes

RESOURCE *Publications* • Eugene, Oregon

EPHESIANS AND ALL THAT JAZZ
Riffing with Paul: A Transliteration

Copyright © 2020 Tom Anderson. All rights reserved. Except for brief quotations in critical publications or reviews, no part of this book may be reproduced in any manner without prior written permission from the publisher. Write: Permissions, Wipf and Stock Publishers, 199 W. 8th Ave., Suite 3, Eugene, OR 97401.

"Scripture taken from the NEW AMERICAN STANDARD BIBLE®, © Copyright 1960, 1962, 1963, 1968, 1971, 1972, 1973, 1975, 1977, 1995 by The Lockman Foundation Used by permission."
www.Lockman.org

Resource Publications
An Imprint of Wipf and Stock Publishers
199 W. 8th Ave., Suite 3
Eugene, OR 97401

www.wipfandstock.com

PAPERBACK ISBN: 978-1-7252-6647-6
HARDCOVER ISBN: 978-1-7252-6648-3
EBOOK ISBN: 978-1-7252-6649-0

Manufactured in the U.S.A. 07/21/20

CONTENTS

Foreword by William Jeynes   vii
Preface   xi
Introduction   xiii

Chapter 1   1
Chapter 2   17
Chapter 3   25
Chapter 4   35
Chapter 5   53
Chapter 6   82

Afterword   108

FOREWORD

Tom Anderson's book, *Ephesians and All the Jazz. Riffing with Paul*, is an amazing and delightful book for a variety of reasons that I will highlight in this forward. However, before diving into this delectable treat, let me highlight two things that are especially worth noting.

First, I have had the joy of knowing Tom for over a quarter of a century and have had the pleasure of having fellowship with him countless times. Over the years, outside of his wife, I have probably become his biggest fan. It is within this context that I had very high expectations of the book. However, he has exceeded them all. Second, you *must* read the first two chapters. These chapters alone are worth a hundred times the price of the book. The theology is rich, understandable and both thought and heart provoking.

The reader will find a number of strengths in Tom's writing. The most notable one is that he has the absolutely exquisite ability to reach people of all spiritual levels. This is huge. Charles Spurgeon declared that this was one of the most essential components of an efficacious gospel presentation. It is so important that in the missionary/evangelistic aspect of the ministry God has given us, we count it one of the highest compliments when people tell us that our preaching reaches the most advanced Christian, but can also be understood by preschoolers. We therefore are quick to perceive the importance of this trait when we see it in others. Such is the anointing of Jesus which He has chosen to share with some of His instruments like Tom.

For example, he speaks to new believers. "You cannot possess Christ without the cross." He also says, "So, when I tell you that you cannot experience real change by coasting and that you must act counter to your natural inclinations, believe me." He writes of truths unbelievers can relate to when he says, "You are totally responsible for your life and what you allow to influence you." Another truth that will open the eyes and minds of unbelievers is, "Those who live in darkness are unaware of His yearning for them since the same shame that blinded Adam blinds them." And Tom reaches the more advanced believer with deep, thought-provoking statements like, "Unless you persuade yourself that you are God-imagined and God-kissed, the real you will continue to hide."

Tom impacts other groups as well. He speaks to married couples when he states, "And since Adam and Eve became self-serving, their relationship with each other became toxic"; and also avers, "And I have the exact same message for you husbands, 'Adapt to your wife!!'" He speaks to those who need a turnaround, "You are the most influential person in your life. You are the best preacher you will ever hear and the best audience you will ever preach to. So, what have you been telling yourself? Anything?"

A second strength of this work is that it can read either as a devotional or a regular book. Given that the book focuses on around one verse at a time in Ephesians, the reader can stop or start at almost any verse. Hence, the book can potentially satisfy the reader who wants to chew on the material and the one who does not like to put books down.

Yet another strength is Tom's use of humor. He threads just the right amount of humor in his book. He makes the reader laugh just enough so that it is a tool used of God without diluting the intensity of the book. For example, he states, "Have you ever sung a duet with your dog?" He uses humor in a balanced way and to make a point. Charles Spurgeon and many of the great preachers used humor effectively as well. He also makes many striking and memorable statements such as, "Jesus' ministry can be summed up in one word—given-ness."

FOREWORD

Finally, Tom Anderson speaks deep truths in a conversational way that resonates with the reader, e.g., "God has saved me. Ho-hum. What's for lunch?" For most of the book, he speaks to the reader like an older brother, repeatedly using the word "you" rather than he, she, we, or they. By the end of the book, the reader will feel like he knows Tom.

Whether you are thinking of a book for yourself, an unbeliever, or a believer, this book is for you. On top of that, this book will draw you into the Word of God in a fresh way which is always a good thing.

William Jeynes,
Missionary/Evangelist, Professor, and Government Advisor

PREFACE

Alexander McClaren was a preacher in the 1800's in England and was a significant voice to his generation. God gifted him to put a fresh face on the gospel message so that his audience could hear the gospel in a way that resonated. In his "Exposition of the Holy Scriptures" he wrote,

> "Now it seems to me that there are very few things that the popular Christianity of this day needs more than a renewing of the familiar old Christian terminology, which has largely lost the freshness and the power that it once had. They tell us that these kerosene lamps, that we are using nowadays, are very much more bright when they are first used than after the mantle gets a little worn.
>
> So it is with the terminology of Christianity. It needs to be re-stated, not in such a way as to take the original meaning out of it, which is what a great deal of the modern craze for re-statement means, but in such a way as to brighten it up again, and to invest it with something of the 'celestial light' with which it was clothed when it first came."[1]

I discovered this quote, written about two centuries ago, after my manuscript was complete and, as I read it, realized that some things haven't changed. Alexander said that the meaning of the

---

[1] Alexander McClaren, "Exposition of the Holy Scriptures" (Amazon ebook)

PREFACE

gospel and gospel words can be defined, but not understood by Christians. Words and concepts like grace, inheritance, righteousness, being filled with the Spirit, the Trinitarian relationship and others can cause one's eyes to glaze over. Even with explanations and expositions, meaning can still remain out of reach.

That is not to lay blame at the feet of either the speaker or the hearer though we do need ears to hear and an anointing to teach or preach. But it could be that the old message, presented a new way, might be just what is needed to awaken both the speaker and listener to these wonderful truths.

I began to write this experiment to fill some time I had. Publishing was not in my thinking. I wanted to explore what I believed and as I wrote, it drew me in. I began seeing more clearly the heart of God and His heart for me. And I was touched by Him. Even now, as I reread this, I say, "wow," and not for what I have put on paper. I say it because the little I've written doesn't even scratch the surface of all that God is and the great love He has for me and His church.

This book can be a new way for you to hear and process God's love for yourself to the end that, hopefully, these concepts become more than just words on paper. My hope and prayer for you is that these words, as our Lord says, become life in you and the God who can seem so distant becomes real and approachable.

INTRODUCTION

Jazz is the best way I can describe what I have written. Jazz is a uniquely American art form and, in its purest form, is improvisation. It takes basic chord structures and then riffs or expresses notes that are imagined, not written.

Jazz is highly subjective and invites the audience to take a journey with the musician as he explores his own soul. At times, it is brilliant. At other times, not so much. Jazz occasionally is not safe. But it is always authentic.

In the first century, Paul was a jazz musician. The good news he proclaimed was uniquely his. He even called the message he preached, "my gospel." What he heard from God was distilled in his own soul before he communicated it to those who were to hear the wonderful love of God.

While Paul was unique in the breadth and depth of the revelation he received, he is not unique in how God transmits His message. Though God can and does sovereignly reveal His Son without human agency, His plan has always been to infect others with someone who has been infected with God.

Paul also talks about two ways to communicate the message. One is by the letter and the other, by the spirit. In musical terms, the letter would be reading from a score and the spirit would be playing jazz. Both require a firm understanding of music theory and an effortless expertise.

INTRODUCTION

While both produce music, however, one is born from within while the other echoes the past and others. John the Baptist, when asked who he was, said that he was a unique voice and not an echo, even though the prophets of old could be heard resounding through him.

Paul said that the Christ he proclaimed was the Christ who was revealed "in" him. The Word that had become Flesh, became flesh once again in Paul. His life and writings were but an outworking of this.

And that Word, in part, has become flesh in me. This work is the result of many years of God changing my thoughts about Him, about myself and about life, and then ultimately changing me. Most of these thoughts I have carried with me for years.

But there were moments when I was writing, that an idea dropped into my mind which had never occurred to me, nor had I heard before. These thoughts are either brilliant or borderline heretical. It felt at those moments as if I was attached to a tether which was being stretched beyond its tolerances. And I let it.

You might sense this as well because jazz at times can have a disrupting effect on one's assumptions and create cognitive dissonance. Jazz can bring unanticipated moments for everyone. But these are the moments when you just might encounter God. Moses did when he stopped to gaze at the incongruent scene of a bush being consumed by fire, yet not burning out. It was in that moment that Moses experienced God in a new way.

With jazz, it is difficult to have the music pause so you can think about what you just heard; but with this, you can. It might be best read in bite-sized chunks so you can consider and pray about the thoughts which might bring a different perspective.

I am asking you to join me in my journey as I try to express the heart and mind of Paul through mine. You will experience some "aha" moments which will create fresh thoughts in you. You also will scratch your head at times (which is equally my hope).

But if you let Him, you will sense the breath of God blowing on you through these pages and find a desire grow in you both to know the God you could never have imagined and the you He imagined before the worlds began. And hopefully at the end, you will find the courage to begin riffing yourself because you too were created to be a jazz musician.

CHAPTER 1

> [1]*Paul, an apostle of Christ Jesus by the will of God, to the saints who are in Ephesus and are faithful in Christ Jesus:*

Paul, sent from Jesus Christ and by God's own choosing, writing to a uniquely positioned people because God has given you two places to live at the same time. Both are of equal importance. I'm writing so that you don't discount either.

The first is right where you live in Ephesus. I know that living there might seem mundane and sometimes cramped; but He has specifically placed you there; and that's what makes it special.

The other address is more real but impossible to discern with your five senses. That is why God has filled you with the spiritual sense of faith so that you can discover, more and more, your real home "in Christ." I will attempt to unpack this as the letter unfolds so you can live well in both.

> [2] *Grace to you and peace from God our Father and the Lord Jesus Christ.*

But to live well in both, your understanding of life must change. The mindset that limits and still plagues some of you is the residue of established thought patterns. In your previous life, you knew deep down that it was all on you to manage and get ahead. Yes, that would include some sort of god or some mantra, like "I think I can. I think I can"; but when it was all said and done, it came down to you and your own efforts.

Life in Christ is the exact opposite. Life now is all on Him and His efforts, and He has included you. Can you see how mind-blowing this is? Grace creates such a disturbance and is so foreign that it takes time to figure out. Many grace bombs will need to drop on your head before it dawns on you.

I hope that when I am done writing this letter, the shock of grace will become amazement and instead of retreating to your own meager efforts, you will be able to rest in His. My purpose in writing is to carpet bomb your mind and heart with one grace bomb after another.

And here comes the first one. The God who has graced you is a Father *and* a Son. He has never needed companionship because this God has always been in relationship, collaborating and working together; playing and enjoying each other. And the favor each shows the other is immeasurable. Sometimes they will even make a game of who can outdo the other. All I know is that the Father is the Son's favorite and the Son is the Father's. They are so keen on each other.

And this favor which radiates from the Father and the wholeness that flows from the Son overflows you. Did you catch that? It would be easy to overlook. What I just said is key to everything I am going to say about our Father and how he embraces you and me. Each one of you is His favorite. I know that this concept is hard to grasp because the term, "favorite," seems to be exclusionary, but not with God.

You are favored because His actions are not determined in the moment, situation by situation. Therefore, you needn't try to determine His mood. The Father loves His Son and everyone associated with Him. And since you are found in Him, there has never been any question concerning God's affections, actions or intent toward you ever.

[3] *Blessed be the God and Father of our Lord Jesus Christ,*

Did I mention that the Father loves His Son? He is so over the top with Jesus that He can't help but laugh. At times, the laughter comes from such a deep place, it sounds like thunder. Yep, that's

CHAPTER 1

Father for you. He gets so tickled being around Jesus since they are so relaxed and have so much fun together. Isn't that how you are with your best friend?

And if I had to describe their relationship in one word, it would be "blessed." It would need, however, a gazillion adjectives to approximate its meaning. And I know that one of those adjectives would have to include the concept of fullness. Everything the Father and Jesus are together fills them so completely that they are ready to burst.

It doesn't take much for His goodness to escape because the Father can't contain Himself. He oozes goodness all the time, and at times, it even explodes from Him. Where do you think I came up with the concept of grace bombs anyway?

And why do you think the Godhead concocted creation in the first place? The fullness of blessing within the Father expands exponentially all the time. Therefore, the Father and the Lord Jesus devised a plan to have an innumerable number of outlets on which grace could be released and create more life.

The problem is, however, that the universe and everything in it cannot begin to contain all that God is. How can the finite house the infinite? This makes me wonder what else God might be doing to fully express Himself.

> *who has blessed us in Christ with every spiritual blessing in the heavenly places,*

But I digress. Let me get back to you. You are such an important part of God's plan because you were created to be the subjective object of His jam-packed love. You were created to be blessed. End of story. You have been brought smack-dab into the middle of God's lovefest because that is the only way they love—up-close and personal. They never love from afar. Theirs always is a bear-hug type of love.

Everything they are and everything they have has already been given to you without reservation. The only reservation is, however, you cannot discover God and what He has just by living a natural life in Ephesus, unaware of Him. No, since these are spiritual and appropriated spiritually, you must learn a new reality.

> ⁴ *just as he chose us in Christ before the foundation of the world to be holy and blameless before him in love.*

That is why you must go back, way back, for this to grip you. You need to be convinced that you are not a mistake, a happenstance or an afterthought. You live so much in the here and now and aware of all the here and now stuff that it's hard to believe that God had you in mind before creation began. But He imagined you from the beginning—you, enjoying both the Bless-er and His blessings forever, and being a conduit of blessing to His world. And to that end, He is working.

> ⁵ *He destined us for adoption as his children through Jesus Christ, according to the good pleasure of his will,* ⁶ *to the praise of his glorious grace that he freely bestowed on us in the Beloved.*

Think about it. He chose you to be on His team before tryouts began. Before He knew you had game (really, before He invented the game), He drafted you. And these two things, His affection and choice, somehow (it makes sense to Him!) makes you an all-star and gives you a seat on the bench next to Him.

If that doesn't blow your mind, this will. He determined long before you arrived on the scene that your relationship with Him would be no different than the one He enjoys with His Son. And it wasn't because He felt sorry for you. He wanted you. In fact, Father was giddy with delight when the thought of having more kids like His Son popped into His mind.

Then when all the legal stuff was finalized by His Son, He threw a party that hasn't stopped yet. And the parties He throws are as over the top as He is. And the gifts! My, my. The gifts. They are indescribable and innumerable, and lavished upon you. All because He knew the unbridled joy that He would have living His life with a whole mess of kids around Him.

> ⁷ *In him we have redemption through his blood, the forgiveness of our trespasses, according to the riches of his grace* ⁸ *that he lavished on us.*

CHAPTER 1

But what a mess we made of it, squandering every opportunity and everything He gave, even selling ourselves into slavery and then blaming Him. Instead of disowning us, He went deeper into His pocket to pay whatever it took to set us free. And after taking us back, never once did any of the shameful things we did ever come up in conversation. It's like it never happened.

But for Him, forgiveness is such a small thing. It might seem big to you, but forgiveness, for Him, is just the beginning. It is the crack in the dam. It is a door ajar. It is a thimble you have dipped into the ocean. Yes, you hold the ocean, but not really. Lift up your eyes.

Forgiveness is the beginning ripples, alerting you to the vastness of His heart surging toward you. Your thimble cannot contain what's coming your way. The tsunami of grace is rushing in to overthrow every structure you have built to hold your life together.

Grace will undo you so you can be done right. And its waves keep coming in, doing what nit-picking and threats, timeouts and punishment can't. They change you. While you play in its surf, His grace changes you.

> *with all wisdom and insight* [9] *he has made known to us the mystery of his will, according to his good pleasure that he set forth in Christ,* *("set forth" in Greek means "publicly displayed")*

Then as you dive in, you will discover that the flow of His grace overwhelms and pulls you in even deeper. The rules and rituals which have kept you tethered to the shore were severed at the cross. For there, God, in plain view for all to see, exposed His true nature, His deep passion and His desire for mankind. On the cross, God in Christ opened His arms wide to draw each and every one into the expanse of His embrace. From the beginning, this has been God's desire; but it took the cross to tangibly express and to fully proclaim the fullness of His heart.

> [10] *as a plan for the fullness of time, to gather up all things in him, things in heaven and things on earth.*

But now, it will take the entirety of time to realize what happened on the cross. I have no clue how He will do it or what it will look like, but nothing, at that time, will resist the attracting power of the cross which is the full expression of His all-consuming love.

The laws of physics which govern the universe will yield to the law which governs His heart. No more resistance. No more friction. No more inertia. No more tension. The entire universe (minus the underworld), both seen and unseen, will flow unrestrained into Him, and the embrace of God will be all-inclusive.

> [11] *In Christ we have also obtained an inheritance, having been destined according to the purpose of him who accomplishes all things according to his counsel and will,*

And at that time, God's affection and appreciation for you will be declared to all in the room. Until then, know that His will has already been signed and is in the hands of the executor. For when God imagined you, He wrote you into His will. And when you came to be, He placed your inheritance into escrow to gain interest.

And now the Triune counsels together to plan the best way to make you ready for such a vast estate. Riches like these have destroyed many so this purposefully is not a gift, but an inheritance. Gifts have the potential to create in their recipients a welfare mentality accompanied by learned helplessness.

God never wants His children to feel like they are on the dole even though His generosity goes beyond their wildest dreams. Therefore, He plans your life so that when His will is finally read, the reasons He gives for bequeathing His wealth are genuine.

> [12] *so that we, who were the first to set our hope on Christ, might live for the praise of his glory.*

And from generation to generation God has been working His plan. Initially, it resulted in some of my Jewish nation living "a pedal to the metal lifestyle" for God, and, in so doing, demonstrating God's wisdom and generosity.

> [13] *In him you also, when you had heard the word of truth, the gospel of your salvation, and had believed in him,*

CHAPTER 1

But now the next phase of His marketing plan is taking shape and He is focusing on you! Imagine! The Clueless with no rhyme or reason to be His are now hearing and believing the message of Jesus and finding themselves included in all that God is doing.

> *were marked with the seal of the promised Holy Spirit;* [14] *this is the pledge of our inheritance toward redemption as God's own people, to the praise of his glory.*

And when you opened the door of your heart, God immediately rushed in to set up shop. Since He is thrilled with every new acquisition, He lit up his sign, "Open for Business" in your front window. (That sign, by the way, is the promised Holy Spirit, God's friend and business partner).

This sign lets everyone know who owns, manages and finances your business. But more importantly, the Holy Spirit guarantees your profitability. You can't even begin to imagine the return coming on His investment. Out of control and ecstatic dance of joy, anyone?

> [15] *I have heard of your faith in the Lord Jesus and your love toward all the saints, and for this reason* [16] *I do not cease to give thanks for you as I remember you in my prayers.*

But now, I need to take a moment to pray. If you have been tracking with me, you know that what I have been saying is way too much to take in at one sitting. Hopefully, however, these grace bombs are accomplishing their purpose and are starting to soften their target.

But to open your heart even more, I must add praying to my preaching. God's sovereignty somehow requires mine, so I choose to pray and pray and pray! But my arm does not need to be twisted because prayer pours out of me.

So when I heard that your faith, like mine, is rooted in Him and that His love has gripped you just as it has me, I haven't stopped including you in my strategic planning sessions with God, thanking Him for you, and bringing you up in our many conversations.

EPHESIANS AND ALL THAT JAZZ

¹⁷ *I pray that the God of our Lord Jesus Christ, the Father of glory, may give you a spirit of wisdom and revelation as you come to know him,*

But before I tell you specifically what I request in our meetings, I want to remind you again with whom I collaborate. I engage the One who embodies glory and who shares the stage with His Son, the Lord Jesus.

This same Jesus has turned that spotlight around on you so that you could glimpse heavenly realities and also understand the process by which He brings about His glory. His greatest glory, by the way, is that you, dust as you are, share the stage with Him. Can you understand how difficult it might be for me to put this into words?

So I need the Spirit's help because the words I use to express what I have grasped are inadequate and shadows at best. And without the Spirit unveiling these things to your heart, regardless of how clearly I communicate, the work of redemption will remain murky. Since the Spirit speaks Spirit-words to your spirit, you and I must connect at that level.

While I grasp for words, I keep asking God to give you the same Spirit that the Father gave to Jesus when He walked the earth. Jesus needed wisdom and insight to navigate life as much as you do. He needed ears to hear in order to recognize His Father's voice. Jesus started from square one just like you. Within the confines of a natural life, Jesus learned how expansive life in the Spirit is because His ears were opened, and He learned the Spirit's language.

How did Jesus come to know who He was? How did He know who His Father was? And how did He know His calling? Him, being God, is not the answer. He left that all behind when He became a zygote. No, He came to realize these things as a real person living in a gritty world.

For sure, His mom and dad told Him that He was special, but it was the Spirit who bore witness to their words in His little heart. And then, as He read and engaged the Scriptures, words and phrases jumped off the page, and He came to realize that His story was hidden and scattered throughout the eternal word. (The eternal

CHAPTER 1

word must be contemporary for it to be eternal.) "In the volume of the book, it is written of me" took on an entirely different meaning when the Spirit lit that up in Jesus' quiet time.

By the way, this is my story as well. For me, it wasn't mom or dad but Barnabas who confirmed me. But ultimately, it was the Spirit who convinced me as He messed with me in the Word. One day I came across this verse, "I have made you a light to the Gentiles to bring salvation to the furthest points of the earth," and it leapt off the page.

I knew that verse was describing Jesus and I began to worship Him. But as I did, I felt that God was pointing to me. I was incredulous. "Are you speaking to me, Lord?" "Me?!" But once I surrendered to what the Spirit was speaking, my life changed, and I had a new trajectory.

The Spirit spoke and I believed. Yes, others acknowledged this calling on my life. And yes, this specific word has been tested time and time again by opposing circumstances (which is one way you can know for sure that it is of God). And yes, it has been borne out as I have pushed myself or maybe as I have been pulled into its call.

These are the ways that I have come to know God better and to know the "me" God imagined before time. But since this process begins and continues with His Spirit, I continually ask God to open my heart more and more to Him.

And my friends, it is no different for you. These things I have just written, is written for all of you, but they must still resonate within. And as for the specifics of your life, God has hidden your destiny in His Word as well, which is all the more reason for your spirit to be tuned to His. So, for this, I am asking.

As you have your eyes open to Christ and see Him more clearly, you will not only come to know Him better; you will also see yourself in a new and glorious light because God-awareness and self-awareness are often coincidental. Yes, you might initially be aware of your imperfections in His light, but as your eyes adjust, you will begin to see your self, as you really are, reflected in His eyes—the beauty He imagined before time.

[18] *so that, with the eyes of your heart enlightened,*

And when you glimpse this, your jaw will drop, and you will slap your forehead. The awesomeness of this revelation will hit you at the same time you think, "Why haven't I seen this before?" This is not a window sort of revelation where you can only look at it from behind a wall. You might get excited about what you see, but it will not change you one stitch.

No, the Spirit's unveiling is an open door which invites you to come in and explore. What God reveals is your permission to enter and make it your own.

you may know what is the hope to which he has called you,

So, I am asking Father for three things to coalesce in your thinking and become the framework into which you fit everything in life. These things have everything to do with Jesus because they belong to Him: His calling, His inheritance and His power. But they also have everything to do with you because you have been included in all the Lord is and has.

The first is that you would know the absolute certainty of His pulling love. Did you know that His love is tugging you into His embrace, into His world and into your future you? God has confidence in His ability to accomplish this and complete faith in you and your inabilities.

His ability and your inability could not be more perfect together. They were made for each other! That is why He brings you to the end of yourself again and again. Your inability is the key, by the way, to discover the Spirit's life animating you. Without being aware of this dynamic, you will flounder in life and misinterpret the very events which are designed to hasten the process.

And I hope you realize that I am not talking about calling, the noun, but calling, the verb. Whether life is booing or applauding, God is both calling you into more of Him and into more of you. In fact, when you realize that He is always calling you, you will know that life doesn't boo at all. Circumstances only echo His call and will cheer you on as you run into His arms.

If you focus on the noun, anyway, you will trip over the perceived tightrope of His will, always concerned about what it might be. However, if you know that He is calling you to Himself in every

CHAPTER 1

moment and through every situation, you will let your guard down as you move toward Him and experiment with life. This is how you discover the noun.

But the noun is also important. So here it is. You are not a maybe. You are an absolute certainty in God's mind. When He imagined you, He named you just like He named the stars, determining your destiny before you began to shine. And there is not a moment when He is not calling you from the confusion of your past into a confident knowing of who you are.

> *what are the riches of his glorious inheritance among the saints, ("among" in Greek is "in")*

Then I am asking God to show you not only who you are, but what you are. Knowing who you are can go to your head. Knowing what you are is a good counterbalance.

You are His safe deposit box. While being special because of its function, one does not go to a bank to "ooh and aah" over an olive-green container. Its value is found within and in its ability to open to its owner. God always puts His treasure in plain wrappers anyway.

And it's kind of crazy to think that God would think of you as a safeguard for His stuff. Of all the places God could put His riches, you and I would not be my first choice. You can see throughout Scriptures how easily we give up what has been given, and you don't need look any further than Adam's interaction in the garden with the serpent. Not even a "let me think about it."

How could God expect a different result from us unless He was confident in His own ability? We will talk at the end of this letter about your part in protecting what He has put in you, but for now, absorb what I am saying and let it absorb you.

God has, in seed form, placed the entirety of what Jesus is to receive within you with the hope that as this seed grows, that which will be His, in whole, will be experienced now in part. That seed is the Spirit who is the atmosphere in which the Father and Son live. The Spirit is envelope in which heaven's culture exists and thrives. And the Spirit is creating heaven's culture here—in, through and among you.

Jesus came to earth to overturn our screwed-up culture and replace it with His. He came to establish His Kingdom. What He and the Father continually experience in the Spirit is the reason for creation and redemption. Because He desires to multiply their "face to face" relationship all over the world, Jesus has poured out His Spirit upon all flesh and has breathed His Spirit into your flesh.

The Spirit who encircles and entwines the Father and Son now immerses you to unite your own heart, and to unite your heart with others. At Pentecost, people of all sorts of backgrounds and cultures came together and grew into one. This is what the Spirit does.

While Jesus came to save individuals, His vision and passion is so much greater than that. In large part, you are a means to an end. I would even say that if saving a bunch of individuals is all that happens, His trip from heaven to hell was largely a waste of time. He came to bring heaven to earth, and that means creating a true oneness in diversity among all people groups, all over the world.

His inheritance, the reward for His efforts, that which has motivated Him from the beginning and what He has deposited in you and me is the Spirit who unites everything in Christ. The Spirit is the Trinitarian thread which ties together the severed parts and pieces scattered all over the world to make them whole and one.

In Christ, heaven is united with earth. God is one with man. The natural and the spiritual coincide. Contrasts that have opposed each other, meld together. Distinctions find their place in the whole. People, with nothing in common, commune. Dissimilar cultures cooperate. Enemies becomes friends. The kingdom of this world becomes the kingdom of our Lord and of His Christ. And a bride. Oh yes, united with His bride! This is His inheritance!!

His kingdom has come within you. Your spirit and His comingle. You find your existence in Him and He exists in you. Deep now calls unto deep and draws you into the same fellowship the Father and Son enjoy in the Spirit.

The kingdom has also come among you. Jew and Gentile are now friends. Rich and poor share meals together. Slaves and masters serve each other. Husbands and wives give their lives to each other. Walls are breaking down and people are tasting heaven because the riches of His inheritance are now being made manifest in the saints!

CHAPTER 1

¹⁹ *and what is the immeasurable greatness of his power for us who believe, ("for" us in Greek is "in" us)*

This is the power of God on display. I know that you have seen some remarkable signs and wonders while I was there, and I hear that God's power is still delivering and healing people. But that power is elementary because demons also can dazzle you with fireworks. Replicating heaven's culture is where real power resides.

The devil can't unite people in love. He can only control through intimidation and fear. Nor do you have the ability within yourself to create a utopia. Heaven knows that this has been tried by various religious organizations and political systems. Each, however, have resulted in an unmitigated failure.

And you needn't look any further than divorce statistics to know that living together in love is not difficult. It's impossible. And that just includes two people. Now add to this, dozens and then hundreds and then thousands. Only heaven's unifying atmosphere can create heaven's culture.

It would be easy for you to discount what God has been doing in your midst. You need your eyes open to see how radical living in community is, and the power it takes to accomplish it. To this end I am praying, so you might see what I see and would know where to direct your prayer efforts. Yes, do pray for miracles, but miracles are best when they are symptoms of God's people living together in unity, rather than one-offs.

Living in community is so important, God is not directing His power toward you with the hope that it influences you. Neither does God just make His power available to you. No, His power is focused, like a laser, into your heart. The seed within must be released from the crusty shell of your soul, and only the power of God can do that.

Your crustiness creates an impenetrable barrier which keeps community from happening. Your preferences, presumptions and prejudices, the way you protect yourself and the things you do to get your way are so much a part of you, it is hard for you to recognize them and their negative effect. Only His power can bypass all of that to convict you of your meager efforts and to accomplish what you cannot.

I know that this is happening in your midst in measure, but you have not yet scratched the surface as to what He really can do in a people who open themselves up to this possibility of God. Wherever Jesus shows up in power and becomes central, the comradery of heaven follows with people becoming friends, and even family.

> *according to the working of his great power.* [20] *God put this power to work in Christ when he raised him from the dead and seated him at his right hand in the heavenly places,*

But don't be surprised at the obstacles and resistance that will line up against forming community. You will have tremendous push back both within and without when you go down this road, as I am sure you have already discovered.

Jesus did when He tried to accomplish this task. Death itself swallowed Him whole and, as you know, death has never given up one of its own, that is, until it met Jesus. And that is, until it met you in Christ.

Death is the undoing of the work of God. It is the tearing of the Trinitarian thread that interweaves all healthy relationships. Restoring severed lives and relationships required a power not yet realized. Though God is known for His power (He is the Almighty, after all), He could not have just waved a magic wand.

The death of Life was required for Life to implode death and reconnect all the relationships that death had severed. Jesus' resurrection established the new order and is now the measure of God's power. Jesus' ascension has now secured it once and for all.

So, when things seem to be falling apart, don't stress. Redemption's power is so great, death is not the end to life, but its beginning. God gave you His ultimate example and answer in Christ, so keep your eyes on Him.

> [21] *far above all rule and authority and power and dominion, and above every name that is named, not only in this age but also in the age to come.*

Not only did God reverse death when Jesus arose, Jesus now sits and rules over all things, even death—especially death. And it doesn't matter whether the death you are facing is physical or

CHAPTER 1

psychological, whether it's broken relationships or broken dreams. Jesus' death, burial, resurrection is the law all things must obey. Life springs from death every single time, regardless how entrenched it seems or how much cement has been poured over the casket.

Did you hear me emphasize the word every? I must reiterate, embolden, underline and add multiple exclamation points to this because it would be easy to relegate God's power to a future date. "Every" means the future for sure, but more than that, it means now.

Jesus Christ and His power has no equal, not now, not ever and so much so that even the mention of His name sets the devil back on his heels. Satan still remembers when Jesus did the David and Goliath thing to him, mano a mano, and saw his entire power structure fall apart. What remains of it is cobbled together with spittle ready to disintegrate at the breath of Jesus.

> [22] *And he has put all things under his feet and has made him the head over all things for the church,* [23] *which is his body,*

But His resurrection also says much about you because God's true relationship with mankind is now revealed. God, in all aspects, became like you, so that you would become, in every aspect, like Him. He exchanged His DNA for yours and, in return, gave you His.

The implications of this are staggering. The angels are still amazed to see the seed that was sown in weakness holding the seat of power. This Man, Christ Jesus, now holds court and every angel and every demon bows to the Man who is God.

They also bow to you because you and Jesus are inextricably entwined. His DNA and Spirit is now yours. Therefore, the myths created about the distant God and the lies told about a miserable mankind have been proven to be as empty as the tomb from which Jesus arose.

While humanity, at the cross, did everything it could to shut God out and while the devil did everything he could to shut Him down, God did everything He could, in the person of His Son, to make His desire to embrace and be embraced by mankind, a reality.

And now, there is no place in heaven or on earth where the truth that a Man and mankind now leans on the Father's chest does not reverberate! Man is co-ruling with God! Every evil spirit, from the little ones who harass you to the big ones who enslave entire nations, is now subject to the Man on the throne and to the God who lives in you.

Cultures cannot keep this out. Dictatorial power cannot drown out this truth. Neither now nor in eternity will Jesus' rule be diminished. The devil might throw a hissy fit from time to time to stir up trouble, but really, hasn't he learned his lesson already?

When Jesus arose, He overturned every law which limited, marginalized and enslaved mankind because God created a new humanity by subsuming every believing one into Himself. He is now your head and you, all of you together, are His body.

the fullness of him who fills all in all.

Everything I have written to this point culminates in this: we, that is, you and me together (this is still incomprehensible to me), are the full expression of His mind, His will and emotions. As a head needs the body to tangibly express its inner thoughts and deepest desires, so God has given us to Jesus.

Without us (I know this sounds heretical), what can Jesus do? We complete Him as much as He completes us. And together, we fill up everything that can be filled up in time and space and eternity. My, oh my!

CHAPTER 2

¹*You were dead through the trespasses and sins*

But to keep this from going to your head, remember that you, like Jesus, were dead, but only dead-er. You see, Jesus was death-scarred because He obeyed God. Your wounds were self-inflicted, stemming from both your stupid ignorance and your outright, in His face, defiance. He, however, agreed to suffer its effects without being its cause.

> ² *in which you once lived, following the course of this world, following the ruler of the power of the air, the spirit that is now at work among those who are disobedient.* ³ *All of us once lived among them in the passions of our flesh, following the desires of flesh and senses, and we were by nature children of wrath, like everyone else.*

I need to paint a vivid picture of what "dead-er" looks like. If I don't, instead of a growing wonder at the astonishing thing God has done, you will just yawn and say, "God has saved me. Ho-hum. What's for lunch?" So, take this word picture I am about to paint and put yourself in the middle of it because, right from the start, you were.

From the beginning, the devil sought to dump his toxic waste in our backyard, and our patriarch co-operated by running to city hall to demand and procure a waiver. And his children, from generation to generation, have fought to keep the swamp from being drained.

And it mattered not that the fumes alone were fatal. We couldn't live close enough to the swamp. We even jumped into the devil's sewage, swimming with our mouths wide open. And whenever we saw a chance to pull someone else in, we did it with glee. We were as toxic as the devil was. At times, he oozed out of us. At other times, he exploded on the scene. Talk about "like father, like son!"

And the death we were was far more repulsive and far more rancid than anything ever imagined: hordes of flies, feasting on putrefying flesh. And the stench was so repugnant that whoever might encounter us would scream, "Run! Run!! Run!!!"

> [4] *But God, who is rich in mercy, out of the great love with which he loved us*

God ran also, but not away from you. He ran right toward you, kneeling to caress and kiss you without gagging or holding His nose. Revulsion turned into compassion because from His deepest part, mercy flows. And when His desire not to harm mixed with His overwhelming desire to do good, He lost control of Himself in the best of ways. Nothing was going to stop Him from rescuing you.

> [5] *even when we were dead through our trespasses, made us alive together with Christ—by grace you have been saved—* [6] *and raised us up with him and seated us with him in the heavenly places in Christ Jesus,*

He rescued you from the fall in such a way that you can never fall again. Creation's kiss was just a peck on the cheek compared with Redemption's. Creation's kiss gave you your own life. Redemption's gave you Another's.

Creation's kiss came with the possibility of death. Redemption's kiss explodes with so much life that death itself creates more life. Creation's kiss brought you to the starting blocks, but with God's rescue in Christ, you begin at the finish line! (Do you see that, by yourself, you can never achieve this, let alone make this stuff up?)

CHAPTER 2

Let me be clear: the rescue God accomplished in Christ so blends your existence with His Son's that distinctions can be made, but barely. He died your death. You live His life. He descended because of you. You ascended because of Him. As Eve was pulled out of Adam to reveal the entirety of Man, you were pulled into Christ to reveal God in all of His glory. Truly you are "bone of His bone and flesh of His flesh."

> [7] *so that in the ages to come he might show the immeasurable riches of his grace in kindness toward us in Christ Jesus.*

And the time is coming when the current heavens and earth will not be big enough to contain the extravagant expressions of Father's ever-expanding appreciation and love for His Son. Once He gets on a roll, watch out! He will have to crumple up the existing universe to create a new one, and then repeat that countless times, just to say, "thank you" to His Son.

And, in a weird way, you and I are the reason that all of this is happening because you gave Jesus the opportunity to show His Father just how far He would go to please Him. And your reward? As Father's creative juices flow, you will not only get front row seats to this extravaganza, but also backstage passes.

> [8] *For by grace you have been saved through faith, and this is not your own doing; it is the gift of God—* [9] *not the result of works, so that no one may boast.*

Whew!!!! Let's catch our breath while I try to encapsulate what I have just put into a nutshell. Talk about a near impossible task! What I have just begun to define for you is salvation from God's perspective, and, as you can see, His salvation is as big as He is.

And I hope that you understand the importance of being on the same page with God. If you begin with a different paradigm, you will only work at cross-purposes. Talk about a recipe for frustration on both sides. That is why it is so important for me to be as clear as I can with you.

God's definition of salvation ought to short-circuit your brain and fry it, not get you thinking about how to curry His favor or to fix yourself or try to put His salvation into some sort of doctrinal box. That sort of thinking is foolish and evidence of pride. To be clear, salvation is being absorbed by Father's favor and wholeness, not changing this behavior or that.

Do you remember how I began this letter by saying that God is filling you with the spiritual sense of faith? In light of the enormity of salvation, can you now see how important this is? The extravagant gift God offers cannot be understood or obtained through your meager mental efforts. You can only comprehend these things by faith.

> [10] *For we are what he has made us, created in Christ Jesus for good works, which God prepared beforehand to be our way of life.*

And a large part of co-operating in the process is knowing that God works from the finished product backwards. When Christ said, "It is finished," He was thinking of you as well. It might feel like you are still on the easel (and you are); but from His perspective, you are hanging on the wall.

Your cooperation is needed, but not finger-painting over the wet areas of your life just because you misinterpret His brushstrokes. Your little part is to rest in Him as you step into the needs around you. The Triune planned these encounters before time in order to add depth and color to your painting. And He is revealing the beauty of His Son in you, one brushstroke at a time.

> [11] *So then, remember that at one time you Gentiles by birth, called "the uncircumcision" by those who are called "the circumcision"—a physical circumcision made in the flesh by human hands—* [12] *remember that you were at that time without Christ, being aliens from the commonwealth of Israel, and strangers to the covenants of promise, having no hope and without God in the world.*

Let me go at this from another angle. Life in Christ is not about being correct. It's about being connected through faith. Even though I talked earlier about the results of your un-connectedness, I don't want you to think that your actions are God's primary concern. I will talk to you later about how cooperating with His Spirit

CHAPTER 2

produces radically different behavior and releases radical blessing; but let's not put the cart before the horse. Connection brings correction and not the other way around.

So remember, before Christ, you, the Clueless, were not connected in any possible way. Even the Jews spewed epitaphs at you. While looking down their nose at you wasn't right, their assessment of you was because, of all people, they understand the concept of "in" and "out." And you were O. U. T.

Psychology 101 says that everyone has an innate desire to be "in" and this manifests itself through two basic soul needs—the yearning to be loved and to feel significant. Outside of Christ, neither are satisfied and as a result, everything you did was either a reaction to not experiencing them, or an attempt to find them. It's no wonder you were a mess.

Before Christ, you never really experienced that gigantic bear hug only experienced in Christ—you know the one that seems to last forever and for no other reason than that you showed up. And there was a gnawing sense in you that, at best, you were a happenstance or, at worse, a big mistake.

There was no destiny written in the stars for you. No wonder you floundered in life. No wonder you were a cynic. No wonder life overwhelmed you!

> [13] *But now in Christ Jesus you who once were far off have been brought near by the blood of Christ.*

But that has all changed now. And you need to celebrate the contrast between who you were and who you are now so this truth can register. You are not just plugged in—you are really in, never to be out again. And words cannot express how close God pulled you into Himself.

I can tell you, however, that you are as close to Jesus as He is to His Father. Jesus, reclining on the Father's chest. Jesus, face to face with God. Jesus in the Father and the Father in Him. With you pulsing through Jesus' veins, it's impossible for you to get closer.

> [14] *For he is our peace; in his flesh he has made both groups into one and has broken down the dividing wall, that is, the hostility between us.*

Therefore, you can put down your weapons and tear down the walls you have erected. Neither fighting nor defending your turf gives you an advantage anymore because you are no longer in a zero-sum game. In Christ, your winning does not require someone else to lose. In fact, your winning only increases theirs and theirs, yours.

Think about Jesus. While the entire world was fighting against him, Christ responded by using peace as His weapon. While we fought, He surrendered. We pushed and He pulled. He unleashed peace's power from the cross, overwhelming chaos with it, making friends out of enemies.

Leading up to the cross, humanity did everything it could to distance itself from Him—from setting up flimsy partitions to waging all-out war. (You can see this still happening today in many quarters.) Our ugly hatred for all things God culminated on the cross where it focused on Him like a laser. The cross became our best attempt to do our worst to God.

But while you were waging war, Jesus was surrendering. And as He opened His arms in surrender, God embraced all of humanity, removing every barrier you erected and every excuse you made.

> [15] *He has abolished the law with its commandments and ordinances, that he might create in himself one new humanity in place of the two, thus making peace,* [16] *and might reconcile both groups to God in one body through the cross, thus putting to death that hostility through it.*

And on the cross, God even removed the only barrier He erected. When he established the Rules, His heart wasn't in them anyway. He knew that the Jews couldn't keep them and, since they were so off-putting, He also knew that the Clueless wouldn't touch them with a ten-foot pole.

Besides, the Rules not only drove a wedge between you and God, it also drove a wedge between those who thought they could keep them, and those who could not care less. These rules were largely the reason the Jews looked down their nose at the Clueless and the reason the Clueless thought the Jews were strange. Talk about sowing the seeds of racism.

CHAPTER 2

This makes what Christ did even more remarkable. In essence, God tore up the old agreement on the cross and re-enacted the one He had in His heart all along. No rules—just the Creator, creating; the Giver, giving; the Uniter, uniting. And with the rules gone, there are no sides to take anyway. With God fully embracing both you and me, how can we not embrace each other?

> [17] *So he came and proclaimed peace to you who were far off and peace to those who were near;* [18] *for through him both of us have access in one Spirit to the Father.*

With the cross behind Him, Jesus has nothing left to do but tell everyone, "The war is over!!" He is so excited, He can't shut up. And it doesn't matter whether you have your back turned from Him or whether you're sitting on His lap, His message is the same: "I want you closer."

If you are quiet enough, you will hear Him. And if you respond, you will discover (along with everyone who is inquisitive) an ease in approaching the Father because the Spirit has come. God's point of access into your life and into everyone's is the same—the Spirit with whom He flooded the earth at Pentecost.

And your point of access into the Father is also the same Spirit because the Spirit doesn't just flow one way. You won't find Him pooling around to eventually evaporate because, simultaneously, the Spirit flows into your heart from the heart of God, and back from yours, into His.

> [19] *So then you are no longer strangers and aliens, but you are citizens with the saints and also members of the household of God,*

So, your connection is not superficial and you are not alone. Distance and barriers are things of the past. Your wanderings are over, and you have come home; but not as another cog in the wheel or as another nobody among a bunch of nobodies.

That is not how Jesus was welcomed home, nor is it how you are embraced. The recognition you receive will make you blush when you realize how important you and your contributions are to Him. But this attention won't puff you up because while the sense of your importance grips you, the enormity of what you have become a part of will overwhelm you even more.

> [20] *built upon the foundation of the apostles and prophets, with Christ Jesus himself as the cornerstone*

And let me tell you, this thing which you are a part of is huge. Just look at the shoulders on which you stand. They are the ones who have had special revelations from God and those who have heard His actual voice. On top of that, and overshadowing all of these, is Jesus. He both under-girds and holds together everything God is doing.

> [21] *In him the whole structure is joined together and grows into a holy temple in the Lord;* [22] *in whom you also are built together spiritually into a dwelling place for God.*

Simply put, God is bringing together the likes of you and me in order to build a magnificent edifice for Himself. On one hand, you don't need the architect present to have your breath taken away by the magnificence of the building. The elegance of the design, the extravagances and efficiencies, the boldness and the subtleties of the structure are enough. Any architect wants His work to speak for itself anyway. He is not so much interested in showing himself off, but his creation. And the building I am talking about is the Church.

But when that building is the architect's own home, the synergy between the house and the owner creates an entirely different experience. While the house reflects his personality, the focus is not on the draperies. They are just the backdrop for Him. This is exactly what God does as He builds us together. He shows us off, while at the same time, we show Him off.

CHAPTER 3

¹*This is the reason that I Paul am a prisoner for Christ Jesus for the sake of you Gentiles—*

When I get caught up in these thoughts, I realize more and more how conflicted I am. Part of me wants to shut myself in with Jesus and worship the Father with Him. And since I want to absorb all He shows me, I find myself hopelessly captivated. To make matters worse, every time I begin to grasp the little He reveals, it leads to something greater. I can't get away from Him, and since I don't want to, being in jail is just perfect for me.

But I also find that I can't escape the fact that when Jesus reveals Himself to me, you are there beside Him. To this day, I cannot see Him without seeing you (or vice versa) and how I desire to show you what I have seen. So it's hard for me to know what to do because I am pulled equally toward Him and toward all the Clueless, but especially you.

> ² *for surely you have already heard of the commission of God's grace that was given me for you,* ³ *and how the mystery was made known to me by revelation, as I wrote above in a few words,* ⁴ *a reading of which will enable you to perceive my understanding of the mystery of Christ.*

You can even see how this has affected my writing. While I am writing to you, but I'm distracted by God. And as I bless Him, I'm thinking about you. I'm such a mess!

So, you must know that whenever God shows me a secret, I am thinking of you. That's why these secrets will not remain secret for long. Whenever God floods my soul with His grace, I am looking for ways to distill His favor in such a way that you can receive it. This is what God has called me to do.

That's why I need to show you how I comprehend His grace, otherwise you will assume that God has His favored few and the few words I have already written will remain shrouded. No!!! My intent in writing is not that you be impressed with my knowledge or wish you had it, but that you are sucked into His vortex of grace.

I have been leaving clues throughout this letter how to get sucked in. Did you notice even in these few pages, how I interact with the God who interacts with me, and that I give away whatever I have been given?

That is the secret. As you read this, think about it and interact with God. Take time to say, "Wow!" And then share whatever insights you get with a friend because revelations mostly begin with little impressions and grow as you express them.

> [5] *In former generations this mystery was not made known to humankind, as it has now been revealed to his holy apostles and prophets by the Spirit:*

And when God's grace grows in you, I will have done my job and will have hope that future generations will enjoy an even greater apprehension of God's overwhelming goodness and favor. Regardless the generation, however, God can only reveal as much as can be received.

Until Jesus came and revealed God's great big heart on the cross, what I have been laying down would have never been received because it is too wonderful. Even the prophets of old danced around the concept of grace because it was too heretical for their time, and I am not sure that they would have believed it anyway. Even though they heard themselves prophesying God's inclusive and forgiving heart, their culture and the law distorted their concept of grace of God.

While there were exceptions, the Jews were caught up in their favored race status, and since they couldn't imagine anything else, it

CHAPTER 3

never occurred to them that all of mankind is the favored race. My brothers in Jerusalem didn't get it either when the Spirit was first poured out, even though Peter prophesied that the Spirit was being poured out upon *all* flesh.

But as Moses was appointed to introduce the law, God is using me to open the door to a grace that reaches everyone. And now others are beginning to see what I see and are leading the charge with both words and action. God's light is flooding the earth, and that light is

> *that is, the Gentiles have become fellow heirs, members of the same body, and sharers in the promise in Christ Jesus through the gospel.*

revealing you, the Clueless! The good news, therefore, is not for a favored few who through nature or nurture have gained a place of privilege, but this good news is for everyone, and especially for those who are as clueless as you.

And I would say the more clueless, the better because when the undeserving, the un-seeking, the un-interested and uninteresting discover God's favor, then grace is really shown to be grace. For me, the cross and the Clueless have become the measure of God's love. The depth of God's love was expressed on the cross, but its breadth is manifest in His reaching out to you.

No longer are the clued-in and the clueless paddling in separate boats, going in different directions. You and I are now fellows in the same ship enjoying the same God, learning the same processes and given the same provisions. Everything promised to the Jewish family now belongs to the all the families of earth because those promises have always been for any who would believe.

> [7] *Of this gospel I have become a servant according to the gift of God's grace that was given me by the working of his power.*

And the grace which rocks the world, rocked mine. In fact, it wrecked me. I was turned on my head when I realized that I was no longer in control of my life. In fact, it was worse than that. I began to realize that my place in life was now as a slave, serving you. This change of thinking does not happen by itself. It took a revelation of the cross and its in-working before these thoughts permeated the depths of my soul.

But when I realized that Christ became less than a slave to reach the likes of me, I figured that I can, at least, become a slave to you. Now it takes constant effort on my part to keep me on track because my natural tendency is to fend for myself. So, I keep praying, "Let me be a servant like you, Jesus."

I don't have time to waste time on things that don't matter. "Let me be just like You" is my prayer every day. And more and more, as I find ways to tell you the astounding news of Jesus' inestimable worth, I find that I am in my attitude, my desires, in my determinations and my abilities.

> *Although I am the very least of all the saints, this grace was given to me to bring to the Gentiles the news of the boundless riches of Christ, and to make everyone see what is the plan of the mystery hidden for ages in God who created all things;*

To think that I, of all people, have been chosen to mirror Jesus! God takes the insignificant and faulty to reveal His glory and perfections. That is what God did with this seemingly "put-together" one. There was a time when I thought that I was the center of the universe because I bought into that nature/nurture thing.

You can imagine how it threw me when I heard "to the Clueless, I am sending you!" Me, a proud Jew, one of the chosen few, called to touch the great unwashed. That caused me to fall on my face before Him, and I wasn't laughing. The Clueless?!

This brought me to the realization that your cluelessness was nothing compared with mine. God's yearning for you was right in front of me all those years, but I couldn't see it. God overturned every thought I had about life and reordered my heart and mind after His. And now to the Clueless I go, telling everyone about this amazing God and His plan.

And God's plan hasn't changed. From the beginning it has been Jesus—all that He is and has!!! Everything was created by Jesus and for Jesus, and nothing is whole without Him. This plan might

CHAPTER 3

have been hidden, but to the hungry heart it was plain to see. It is only hidden from those who think that being "put together" is a badge of honor, and therefore, don't need God.

Jesus showed how full an empty man could be when He emptied Himself and lived life as an empty vessel. While being poor and needy often shames us, it was the Son of man's glory because, from the beginning, need has defined humanity.

God created the angels with no need. They are glorious in their own right, and they excel in strength. Angels are like energizer bunnies who just keep going. They don't sleep. They don't eat. They don't poop. They were created to exhibit the awesomeness of God's mighty power.

God created you, however, with *all* need and were made to excel in weakness. This was God's plan even before the fall. You were created to rely on Him, with need being both the means to discover Him and the impetus to call on Him. While sin added another layer to need, your need is not evidence of the fall. It reveals your design. You were made with holes that could only be filled with Jesus. And God's power rests on those who embrace their need.

So don't buy into the devil's lie that you have to be put together. You were made undone and will remain undone until you die. Your need is your point of contact with the Living God. In fact, I say, "The needier, the better." Felt need is one of greatest gifts God can ever give. So, embrace your need and

> [10] *so that through the church the wisdom of God in its rich variety might now be made known to the rulers and authorities in the heavenly places.*

embrace your design! Your lack and inability gives God an opportunity to display His wisdom and power. And He's not just looking to prove Himself to you because God had something to prove to Satan and his ilk who concluded that God was a bit doddery. (Why else would Satan think that he could take the throne?)

So, God made creatures who were really weak and very foolish to show the supposed powerful ones how wrong they were about everything. And to remove any doubt, God dressed up as a fool Himself by becoming human. And, to cap it off, Jesus now multiplies weakness exponentially by gathering all the weak ones to Himself. And pointing to you and me, He tells Satan, "Look what I can do!"

> [11] *This was in accordance with the eternal purpose that he has carried out in Christ Jesus our Lord,*

In light of our constant failures, Christ becoming a man and embracing the cross might seem like a backup plan, but it wasn't. It was the plan from eternity. It only came to the forefront after the devil thought he won. God's preference has always been to reveal His glory in a show of weakness.

Anyone, including the devil, can win some points through bluster, but hearts cannot be won by force. So, the Lion who is a Lamb at heart stepped into time to reveal His true self through a display of approachability, rooted in humility and vulnerability. You cuddle a lion at your own risk, but not a lamb.

And for the Triune, this was no act. Lucifer mistakenly got caught up in the pomp and glitz of the throne and wondered why God was not interested in any of it. Because Lucifer set His heart on the glitter, he lost sight of the One who would rather wash someone's feet than sit enthroned. In so doing, Lucifer lost his true self.

> [12] *in whom we have access to God in boldness and confidence through faith in him. ("faith in Him" in Greek is "the faith of Him")*

Before I flip the emphasis of this letter, I want to highlight what I have been saying to this point and explain its implications. You will discover and live out your true self when you come to believe what He believes about you. This must begin with the revelation that you have been subsumed in Him.

God loves the you He made and wants you to know that person. But you won't be able to unless you realize that, in Christ, you are tucked into the folds of God. As this dawns on you, oh, the freedom and the confidence it will bring. Your approach to God and to life will be more and more effortless as you come to know the you God created.

CHAPTER 3

You see, being "in Christ" is not a static doctrinal position. It is dynamic and vibrant. It propels you. Being "in" allows you to go "into." Don't forget that. Use your favored position to gain more access.

And I now need to come full circle. Since I began this section with faith, I am going to end it with faith because nothing works without it. You cannot enter the spaciousness of God through the portals of your mind or by trying to believe. I hope, by this point, you are starting to grasp this.

So. it is not about trying to muster up faith or putting *your* faith in God because there is only one faith, and that would be His. You must learn to receive His faith and live by it because you live, if you live at all, by Jesus' faith. This is only realized when you discover the exchanged life—no longer I, but Christ. Your natural faith will not cut it because the faith of the Son of God is not rooted in your soul, but in Himself and in your spirit.

> [13] *I pray therefore that you may not lose heart over my sufferings for you; they are your glory.*

I'm telling you this because I've heard that you have been trying to keep your faith since you heard of my condition. Since it's hard to put what I am going through into a blessing box, some of you are doubting God's goodness. Don't! I have been able to take advantage of my imprisonment because I have exchanged my confusion for His clarity, my weakness for His ability and my faith for His.

Case in point: do you hear a man in restraints as you read this? Hardly. My world is big and growing. In fact, some of the very things that I am writing to you has dawned on me here. So, when you hear the "woe is Paul" reports from other people, don't believe it.

No one around me does. In fact, I overhear them say to each other, "Paul's pain is our gain," in order to keep their spirits up. I chuckle when I hear this because it's true. But I also know that they are embracing this same attitude when they go through it, and this encourages me as well.

> [14] *For this reason*

EPHESIANS AND ALL THAT JAZZ

What I have said about being in Christ turns everything on its head and challenges every basic assumption you have about life. But now I am going to release another bomb which will cause even more befuddlement. These bombs are designed to destroy the faulty foundations of your life so that your life can be built on grace.

To this point, I have been laying the foundation of you being "in Christ." Your situations do not define you, neither does your past. You, being in Christ, does. This is God's perspective on who you are and your potentiality, and as you embrace it, everything will change about you and for you.

But being "in Christ" is not the only thing God wants you to know because God is not just interested in changing you. He has the world in His sights and knows that in your own strength, you cannot affect any change; but "Christ in you" can. This is God's one-two punch—You in Christ, and Christ in you.

Jesus has always been the Father's answer. Jesus died as your substitute and now lives as your replacement. So, while Jesus will remain my subject, my emphasis will change. I want to alert you to that before I begin so you can continue to track with me.

> *I bow my knees before the Father,* [15] *from whom every family in heaven and on earth takes its name.*

And that is why I must pray again. "Father, I am awestruck. You see everything through the prism of Your relationship with Your Son and this, more than anything, has brought me to my knees. I thought for all those years that "Hear oh Israel, the Lord, our God, is One Lord" meant nothing more than singularity—that "God alone" meant that God was alone. But when I met Jesus, my world turned upside down! I realize now that You has always lived in community and I can hardly fathom it.

On top of that, You are in an ever expanding community, having created families I can see, and families I can't. Thank you that you have destined each and every relationship to reflect Yours; and You do this by injecting Yourself into them.

> [16] *I pray that, according to the riches of his glory, he may grant that you may be strengthened in your inner being with power through his Spirit,*

CHAPTER 3

But Lord, the structures we have created, our theologies and assumptions, are neither big enough nor strong enough nor flexible enough to house Christ. They only restrict Him.

So, thank You for creating within each of us a God-designed container. Spare no expense to make us aware of this; and strengthen the God-part of us by Your Spirit. Explode our thinking so we can be the sort of structure able to contain Your expansive nature,

> [17] *and that Christ may dwell in your hearts through faith, as you are being rooted and grounded in love.*

for only then, Christ can make His home in us. Remodel and repurpose as You desire, but especially attend to the basement. It is, for many, still dark and damp and suspect because they remain unconvinced of Your love. So, let Your love invade the dark places of our lives. Root Yourself in our failings and inadequacies, and establish us upon Your grace.

> [18] *I pray that you may have the power to comprehend, with all the saints, what is the breadth and length and height and depth,*

Since You neither intend to live in a one-room shack nor repose in a finished mansion, keep knocking down walls. Your house plans are as expansive as You are. Shatter our prejudices and widen our narrowness. Stretch our thought life to the heavens and touch our emotions at its depths. You have created us to expand in every way

> [19] *and to know the love of Christ that surpasses knowledge, so that you may be filled with all the fullness of God.*

so we can fully engage the Father like Christ does, see ourselves through His eyes and transform others with Your touch. Lord, this type of knowing goes beyond anything I could ever imagine. It is as different as knowing a frog by dissecting it or knowing a frog by being it. Father, help us "be," but especially help us be as pregnant with You, as Christ is."

> [20] *Now to him who by the power at work within us is able to accomplish abundantly far more than all we can ask or*

> *imagine,* [21] *to him be glory in the church and in Christ Jesus to all generations, forever and ever. Amen.*

My friends, please don't fall into the trap that says God's presence and provision is for a future date. God's expanding fullness is yours now. And don't think that He comes in dabs and dribbles either. Exceedingly. Abundantly. Excessively. These words don't even come close. In fact, words fail when God shows up.

Keep asking God for the very things I am. He has already said yes to them. And then let your imagination go wild for that is part of the process of prayer. My faith ignites when I stretch the limits of my thinking, considering how God might do the impossible. He surprises me every time.

But I have also learned not to look for answers to fall from the sky, because His power is working in me. I expect to be a significant part of the answer to my prayers.

Even though I am the instrument people hear, however, I will not toot my own horn. He is the one who has written the score, and He is the one both playing and conducting the music. He is the one who deserves the standing ovations and the curtain calls.

And since Jesus is always the first one to jump to His feet to shout, "Maestro! Maestro!" to His Father and ours, may the church follow His lead with a crescendo of praise, both now and in every generation, to endless days. Make it happen, Lord!

CHAPTER 4

> [1]*I therefore, the prisoner in the Lord, beg you*

Fair warning. I'm getting ready to meddle. I must. Being in Christ and having Christ alive in you, as I have said, challenges every basic assumption you have about life. Since these concepts are so otherworldly and elusive, many come up with their own version of the Christian life and declare it to be God's, only to defend it to death or wither to death.

So, I am going to beg. I'm going to cajole. I'm going to exhort. I am going to reason with you. I will even command. I will do almost anything so you can discover His version of the Christian life.

And you can be in no better classroom than the one that you are in right now. God does not waste anything—certainly not your confines or circumstances. I know that He hasn't wasted mine! What He teaches me spiritually is fleshed out in the bumps and grinds of my life, and I have learned to embrace these God-imposed limitations. And the trick for you to figure out the seeming incongruities of your Christian life is to accept yours as well.

Look at me. I am the King's kid, yet I'm in prison. You too are both royalty and equally limited in other ways. Don't you remember that I began this letter by telling you that you lived in two worlds and that I wanted to help you figure out how to live well in both?

> to lead a life worthy of the calling to which you have been called, ² with all humility and gentleness, with patience, bearing with one another in love,

As you have discovered, living Christ's life is Ephesus is not an easy equation to figure out. Your Teacher, however, has confidence in you, and He's called you to the front of the class to work out each step on the blackboard.

So, keep your head up while puzzling through this problem. He knows the answer is right below your conscious level, and as you work and rework the answer on the board, you will get it.

But offset the pride of being chosen with a humble heart. The complexities of living Jesus' life have made fools of many who assumed that just because they figured out a step or two that they have really solved it. The enormity of this problem must first bring you to your knees before it reveals its answer.

Be aware, also, that the Teacher has called the entire class to the blackboard. He knows that this equation is bigger than any one person and expects you to collaborate with each other. So don't hide your figuring from them, especially when you don't seem to get it. Dialogue and pray together. This is exactly how the answer is worked out. And feel free to look over their shoulders as well because cheating is allowed in His classroom. Their insight will be key to unlocking your own.

> ³ making every effort to maintain the unity of the Spirit in the bond of peace.

And I chuckle when I think that God has put all of us together to work through this problem because we are such territorial and competitive creatures. Being in close confines triggers all sorts of lovely things in us. So here we are, working with people who get on our nerves! Ha!

This is especially funny because the answer to the equation is one. $1 + 1 = 1$; $1 + 2 = 1$; and so on. A simply elegant statement of fact—one only the Triune could conceive! And He gives the answer upfront so that you can work backwards toward the solution.

For the unifying nature of the Spirit has been on display in the Godhead from the beginning. The Father and the Son, who are Two

CHAPTER 4

make One. And then add the Spirit Himself to make Three, but all Three together equals One.

Puzzling for sure, but beautiful. The Spirit, like a great Puzzle Master, fits everything together in such a delightful way. This one plus that one plus another one, ad infinitum always adding up to one. And for Him, it's easy-peasy.

But this has not been so easy for you or for me because this hasn't been our experience. For us, one plus one has resulted sadly in division and conflict and hurt. While this equation was designed to make everything and everyone whole, our best efforts have resulted in feeling apart, against and alone.

But the Holy Spirit is come! He is the One who has forever enveloped the Father and Son in His enchanting vapor, making their perfect relationship even more delightful. His unifying nature is the atmosphere in which you now live, my friends, with your friends.

So, breathe deeply and breathe often, and you too will come under His spell. Your minds will clear when you see the simplicity of the solution. Once that thing which you have been working out is worked out in you, your striving will cease. And the inward sense that the Holy Spirit makes sense and integrates our various takes on Scripture will allow you to relax and work together with unguarded hearts.

> [4] *There is one body and one Spirit, just as you were called to the one hope of your calling,* [5] *one Lord, one faith, one baptism,* [6] *one God and Father of all, who is above all and through all and in all.*

Therefore, let's not quibble over the different ways Scriptures can be interpreted. The potential for differences is not accidental, but by design. (There are over 1000 varieties of bananas, for goodness' sake.) God has put enough in Scripture to counterbalance most positions you hold. He has done this, not to bolster your arguments, but to reveal your heart.

It comes down to this. Do you want to be right and spend your time trying to convince everyone else that you are, or do you want to work together with your brothers and sisters to impact the world? Remember what I said about correctness and connectedness? This is what I meant.

I hear this all the time—saints getting caught up in how the church is organized and operates, rather than being the church. Or taking sides over how the Spirit does or does not work, instead of walking in the Spirit. Should I go on? Does Jesus' Lordship only mean following rules? Is faith passively trusting God or can I "name it and claim it"? And I cannot even begin to tell you the issues that baptism presents. Are you beginning to see how these things might divide?

That is why I have come to a couple conclusions. First, in most matters, we need to walk softly because we are better served when we understand most differences as both/and, and not either/or. On some level, the Holy Spirit synthesizes our seemingly incompatible Scriptural viewpoints into a symphony of faith and love. Besides if your theology is not evolving, it is a fossil.

But more importantly, instead of focusing on what divides, celebrate the Father together because we are ever in His embrace. Doctrine cannot create identity and culture; only the Father can.

So, beloved, embrace the Father together! I know you are more comfortable in one group or another, but that does not mean you need to demonize or marginalize the other. He has birthed each group and cares for all of them.

In fact, the more you can bridge that gap, the more you will be surprised by His presence. The Father has determined to reveal Himself to His creation through many "yous." So, if you keep others at arm's length, you will keep Him and His work at bay as well. But as you extend your hand to them, regardless their doctrine, you will discover that He has hidden Himself in them for you to find.

> [7] *But each of us was given grace according to the measure of Christ's gift.*

But this works both ways. God has also hidden Himself in you for others to find. As Jesus was the Father's gift, so you are Christ's gift waiting to be unwrapped. Jesus allowed Himself to be unwrapped by stepping into the needs He encountered. The love of God was revealed layer by layer as Jesus opened His heart more and

CHAPTER 4

more. You too will find your unique voice and ministry as you step into need; and when you do Christ will once again be unpackaged.

> [8]Therefore it is said, "When he ascended on high he made captivity itself a captive; he gave gifts to his people."
> [9] (When it says, "He ascended," what does it mean but that he had also descended into the lower parts of the earth?

Jesus' ministry can be summed up in one word—given-ness. Jesus is the gift of God who came to lavish gifts upon mankind so that anyone who receives Him will become a gift as well. Gifts stacked upon gifts creating more gifts when opened! And now, seated on high, He is in the position to be wildly generous.

But until His people were able to appropriate them, these gifts remained wrapped. And until His people were gathered up, the Father could not enjoy them. What a two-fold conundrum. Since the enemy held the Father's treasure in his lair and in darkness, Jesus needed to enter the dark recesses of the earth to retrieve them.

Jesus could not idly stand by and do nothing because, while Jesus' love for mankind was great, His love for the Father is unsurpassed. The Father's longing was the deeper need which compelled Jesus to go deeper still. The cry of His Father's heart to be reunited with mankind compelled Jesus to leave heaven in order to destroy the enemy's seat of power and prove His Lordship.

Jesus used the physicality of a human life to stage His assault on hell. Since the portal into the underworld was death, Christ took on flesh to go through that gate. While Jesus walked among us, the devil took pleasure animating the ones who were created for life to be weapons of death. This culminated on the cross where Death dealt Life a death blow and then swallowed Him whole.

Little did the devil realize, however, that this bloodied and battered Christ was, in fact, the real Trojan Horse. With glee, the devil brought the seemingly discarded package into his inner chambers to gloat. But he discovered his strategic blunder too late and has rued that day ever since. To think that the deceiver himself was deceived. Brilliant!!

The Gift was unwrapped. Jesus was revealed to be Savior, Deliverer and Lord, and forever more will be known this way. Blinding light shone in the darkness. The chains were loosed. The band started playing and the victory march began. And all the devil could do was cower in the light with his eyes covered.

When the parade ended at the throne of heaven, the Holy Spirit was mustered in full battle array to equip the devil's former captives with weapons and provisions, in order to lead them in the mop up action.

> [10] *He who descended is the same one who ascended far above all the heavens, so that he might fill all things.)*

(This is Jesus, the Father's darling and mankind's champion! No greater love story has ever been written. Jesus dove into the depths of darkness to open the floodgates of heaven. He released the pent-up emotions of the Father and nothing can stand in the way of His love-surge. It overflows everything!)

> [11] *The gifts he gave were that some would be apostles, some prophets, some evangelists, some pastors and teachers,* [12] *to equip the saints for the work of ministry, for building up the body of Christ,*

With the influx of recruits volunteering for the Spirit's mission, envisioning and training became essential. Leaving nothing to chance, Jesus equips some in each generation to train others and lead the charge.

A full team of specialists is required to accomplish this gargantuan undertaking. Strategists and motivators must oversee the work and keep it on point. The recruiters need to keep on recruiting while teachers and hands-on trainers work closely with those who sign up. When functioning as Jesus drew it up, it works beautifully.

Since the goal is a cohesive, battle-strong army, these leaders must focus on both team building and individual strength training. Creating strong individuals who are even stronger team members is tricky because recruits must be able to think on their feet while knowing how to follow orders.

And there are some key indicators which show that this mentality is forming. First, the recruits will have a personal relationship with the General and will see their small part as an expression of

CHAPTER 4

their devotion to Him. Then, when corporals begin to take privates under their wings without being asked, we are well on our way.

> [13] *until all of us come to the unity of the faith and of the knowledge of the Son of God, to maturity, to the measure of the full stature of Christ.*

When it is all said and done, we rag-tags will function with one heart and mind. That is why the Holy Spirit is not as interested that you are on the same page doctrinally as He is with you personally taking steps of faith each time more of Jesus is revealed.

You can easily deceive yourself by thinking that because you know something intellectually, you possess it. You must continually unite your knowing with faith actions because God has invited you to enter His world, not just observe it. So, it doesn't matter whether you are an academic or a janitor because the fullness of life in Christ is open to anyone who responds to Jesus by taking little steps of faith.

Knowledge was never meant to be academic because knowing what He knows sparks adventures. And faith was never meant to be presumptuous because His sort of faith springs from and is intimately connected with sensing what the Son of God knows. And, as I have said before, what He knows about you, about His Father and about every aspect of life is exponentially greater and far more wonderful than your most far-flung thoughts.

When you embrace this lifestyle, you will find yourself fully embracing the "you" God created without comparing yourself with anyone else. This is a mark of maturity. You will also fully discharge your duties without doubting yourself. And with each passing generation, this unfolding knowledge of Christ will produce in His people an ever-increasing faith until, at last, He sees His mirrored image in us without distortion.

> [14] *We must no longer be children, tossed to and fro and blown about by every wind of doctrine, by people's trickery, by their craftiness in deceitful scheming.*

But make no mistake. Entering His world is not for the faint of heart. Life in Christ is fraught with danger. And one of the greatest dangers spring from your own immaturity and lazy thinking. Some who enlist in His army secretly hope that others will fight their battles for them and some choose to fight alone. If this isn't addressed head on, it will be difficult to win any skirmish.

Can you imagine entering a battle without first being hardened and sobered through basic and advanced training? I don't need to be a prophet to predict that outcome. And I can't tell you the number of Christians who saunter into mine-fields because they see something that glitters, totally unaware of the danger and so unprepared.

Some get thrown this way and others get thrown that. On top of this, they are oblivious to the snipers who have their sights trained on them or the infiltrators who have put on the uniform to lead the troops astray.

Listen, I expect children to be clueless and chase after baubles, not those with some smarts. So, let me be direct. Every time the Spirit reveals a little more of Christ to His people, some are there to capitalize on it by packaging it. What was intended to sweep His people into the arms of God and then into the world instead becomes a self-aggrandizing, self-improvement movement.

And the unsuspecting grab their surfboards, hoping to catch a wave, only to find themselves floundering among the sharks. With all the various movements coming and going, I sometimes think that the only movement the church needs is a good bowel movement.

[15] *But speaking the truth in love*

So, if anyone offers you junk food and calls it a balanced meal, or if anyone separates the warm fuzzies from hard realities, run away from them as fast, and as far, as possible. You cannot possess Christ without the cross. As Christ needed to enter a hell hole to get the spoils, you too must face hard truths about yourself before you can apprehend the beauty that is you.

At times, you will sense your perfections and be ecstatic. At other times, you will be brought to your knees, overwhelmed with your imperfections. But knowing the truth of God's love will keep you grounded through these ups and downs and will help you grow.

CHAPTER 4

His love is the soil in which you are rooted and from which you spring. His love is the antidote for shame, that sense of not measuring up, which keeps His glory from shining through you. Look, I'm speaking truth to you. Do you hear it? You are wrapped in the love of God. Is that how you see yourself

> we must grow up in every way into him who is the head, into Christ, [16] from whom the whole body, joined and knit together by every ligament with which it is equipped, as each part is working properly, promotes the body's growth in building itself up in love.

because this is how you, each one of you, are? I would even go so far to say that "wrapped in His love" does not go far enough because the wrapping is something other than you. No, you are the embodiment of all that He is. While your body can be considered its own entity theoretically, it's impossible to do that practically. You are as much your body as you are not.

A body was provided for Jesus so that the invisible God could be seen. The immaterial God could touch and be touched. The holy God could become approachable. The distant God could hug. The impervious God, cry. The eternal God, die. Without a body, God is just a distant theory. But with a body, God comes into focus. And, in each generation, a body is provided for Him and that body is you!

What Christ accomplished in His physical body a couple thousand years ago is nothing compared with what He desires to do in it now. You individually, and all together, give expression to who He is because He is the One animating you. But for this to happen, you need to (as every cell in your body intuitively knows) receive His life daily, respond more and more to the impulses of His Spirit and interact with the cells around you.

He has fit you into the most sophisticated organism ever created. It is comprised of many systems organized into a cohesive whole, and exists to validate itself and affect its environment. To find your place there is the most exciting thing you can do, and the most important.

EPHESIANS AND ALL THAT JAZZ

> [17] *Now this I affirm and insist on in the Lord: you must no longer live as the Gentiles live, in the futility of their minds.*

In light of this, what I'm about to say can't be said strong enough. In fact, (and I don't do this often) I am going to invoke the Lord because it is so important. For God's sake, don't be clueless!! Your behavior doesn't just affect you. It affects His entire body.

Unless you are first broken and then mended by Him, your instincts will deceive you and, just like the Clueless, will hurt the cause. That is why my tone has changed and I am taking a much tougher stance. Parables and subtleties might draw you toward spiritual realities, but they will not get you out of the gutter.

So, if I offend, that is my intent. You need to get off dead center and fully commit yourself to Him and His body because without intentionality, you will be as undisciplined and oblivious as the Clueless. They think they are doing all right as they slide toward hell.

> [18] *They are darkened in their understanding, alienated from the life of God because of their ignorance and hardness of heart.* [19] *They have lost all sensitivity and have abandoned themselves to licentiousness, greedy to practice every kind of impurity*

You see, they live in a vicious cycle. Because they have no connection to the Spirit's realm, they can only seek gratification from their own perverted world where they consume all sorts of crap and call it a feast.

This is how it works. Because they have never experienced real beauty, beauty is redefined to mean anything which makes then feel good. It begins innocently enough, but as these thoughts are acted upon, desire increases. As they consume more of their desires, addiction grabs hold of them and begins to consume them.

At this point, it does not matter what anyone thinks. Whether it's drugs or making a name for themselves, getting a fix becomes all-consuming with nothing getting in their way and with more, never being enough. Regardless how refined the addiction, that beast grabs hold and rules with an iron fist. And, more and more, they are driven to its ugliest and filthiest slop-holes, totally unaware of what is happening.

CHAPTER 4

> [20] *That is not the way you learned Christ!* [21] *For surely you have heard about him and were taught in him, as truth is in Jesus.*

And if you are unaware of spiritual realities, (that is, how God interacts with you and how you apprehend Him), you too will remain in default mode and, like the Clueless, never discover the secret of life in Christ. From childhood, you developed some deeply ingrained thoughts and reactions to life that have become second nature. The things you did over the years to protect yourself and control your world were touted as personal strengths.

Since God has wired you to feel safe, you did, at that time, what you could to protect yourself. Depending on your personality, you might blow up or withdraw, and some of you still do. Without personal awareness, however, you will continue to sabotage yourself and mess up others. What most Christians don't realize is that these hurtful patterns of living passed through regeneration unscathed, and the things you did to protect yourself before, continue to afflict others and cause strife after, that is, until you come to the end of yourself.

Yes, when you received Christ, all things became new, but not in the sense that your behavior was magically changed or blessed. The large implication of "all things becoming new" is the need to relearn everything. This is a painful process which takes you out of your comfort zone. Knowing about Christ is safe; learning Christ is not

> [22] *You were taught to put away your former way of life, your old self, corrupt and deluded by its lusts,* [23] *and to be renewed in the spirit of your minds,* [24] *and to clothe yourselves with the new self, created according to the likeness of God in true righteousness and holiness.*

because the residue from your old patterns of behavior is exposed when you follow Him. At least that is how it was for Jacob and Peter, and for me. Behaviors can be so automatic that without self-awareness, you can live way below your potential and act in ways that continue to hurt yourself and others. And your default mode will fool you every time.

I can use several analogies to help you understand the process of becoming more like Christ. One is going on a journey and another is getting dressed, though I'm sure that there are others.

To journey anywhere, the appeal of your destination must be greater than the place you reside. At times, where you live might not seem that bad, but seeing the beauty of somewhere else is all you need to start making plans to leave. Figuring out how to get there is secondary because once you decide to leave, you will take out a map.

It's the same for getting dressed. You must realize that your clothes need to be changed before you will reach for a fresh set. In either case, you must find motivation to change. You can become so comfortable where you are and accustomed to the you that you were. You need to be able to smell what others do. The best way to do that is to bury your nose into some freshly washed laundry. Then you will know and will be motivated to change your attire.

> [25] *So then, putting away falsehood, let all of us speak the truth to our neighbors, for we are members of one another.*

Because it is difficult to look at yourself impartially, God has put brothers and sisters around you. Take advantage of this. Instead of being reactive and defensive, invite your friends to be honest with you. You need the Spirit's help and the help of those closest to you because you have blind spots.

Itemize the behaviors which undermine true relationships and each time you see them raise their ugly head acknowledge it while telling yourself that this behavior does not define you, because it doesn't. I had to do this for years because the root of my self-life went deep.

It took many hard knocks to get me to think straight for I was the big man on campus before I headed to Damascus and acted like it. After I encountered Jesus, I continued to act the same way. What I did to exert my will on the world and get my way before I encountered Christ, I did after. Only my subject and audience changed.

I still argued with the best of them. I was so sure of myself and spoke in such a forceful manner that no one dared tell me that I was

CHAPTER 4

full of myself. I was Saul, the Pharisee, who now had Jesus! I didn't know, however, that I was lying to myself and to others.

For while what I said was true, it wasn't the truth because truth will draw the hungry into His loving embrace even if it has a hard edge to it. But when I was around, people were cowed into silence and wanted to stay away or send me away.

That's really what happened to me in Damascus. I knew that I was right and everyone was going to know it, whether they liked it or not. The saints finally had enough of the trouble I caused and "helped" me escape with my life. However, they were really helping themselves because they wanted to escape from me. They said, "Too much Saul" after I left.

Then when my brothers in Jerusalem saw the effect that I had on everyone there, they had enough as well and told me to leave. I heard later that, after I left, there was a huge sigh of relief and the church came alive again and began to grow once more.

That was hard for me, but I am so glad they had the courage to confront me because I would have continued to be a pompous ass. (When I told you about talented people hurting the church, I was talking about myself.) This has been one of the most important lessons of my life. I could have gotten angry with them and went somewhere else to prove them wrong. But that would have just created another crisis in a different group.

Thankfully, I directed my anger toward Jesus and had it out with Him. But the madder I got, the quieter He became until I was quite spent. Then I realized that Jesus was the One sending me to a time out, and this shattered my world.

It hit me that I was attacking those outside of the church with the gospel in the same way I had attacked the church with the law. This hindered God's work more than when I was a Pharisee. At least then, my persecution caused the church to spread and grow. All it did now was turn off the saints and harden the world against the gospel.

I lost all my bearings and became unsure of myself, my calling and my relationship with the Lord. The only thing I knew at that time was, regardless how gifted, I was of no use to anyone in my condition.

Then it dawned on me what I needed to do. Since I was argumentative and needed to be in the limelight, I had to go somewhere and be alone to let Jesus heal my heart. I didn't want my natural abilities to control me anymore. It took three years to have the fight taken out of me, but since then, all I have wanted is to get out of the way, desire Him and what He wants, and as importantly, to have His will done His way and in His time. I, Saul, the self-assured, became Paul, the small.

So, when I tell you that you cannot experience real change by coasting and that you must act counter to your natural inclinations, believe me. It's hard work from start to finish. First, you must be honest with yourself which might be the hardest part of all. Then you must resist acting in default mode by intentionally doing the opposite. Ouch! But what I have discovered is that as I took these steps of faith, Christ stepped up in me.

For example, if you tend to lie, whether you are purposefully being deceptive or just hiding shameful behavior, get it out in the open. Find someone who has gone through the meat grinder and has come out sweet sausage to hold you accountable. Why do you think you have brothers and sisters?

Be brutally honest, knowing that you are not going to change overnight. But you will, and when you do, you will sense a new freedom, and others will seek you out to help them with the same process.

> [26] *Be angry but do not sin; do not let the sun go down on your anger,* [27] *and do not make room for the devil.*

If you get angry easily, the same thing applies. An angry person is going to explode when stressed or crossed. It's an automatic reaction. But as soon as you do, tell God that you are angry. And you might, like I did, need to get alone with Him and vent. If you are honest with your feelings, it is not a sin, but if you direct it toward someone else or nurse it, it is.

And before you are done fuming, give up any right you might think you have. Thinking that you are owed something and not getting your way is at the root of most anger. Acknowledge that you use your anger to control others and to get your way, and then ask

CHAPTER 4

for forgiveness. Also give permission to those who know you best to call you out when you do react.

There are many ways to hand the devil control of your life and to destroy relationships, but anger is one of the most direct. This emotion gives voice to the devil's rage against God and to his hatred of others. Is that who want to channel? When your anger is directed toward others, demons rush in behind your violent assault to rub salt in your victim's wounds.

> [28] *Thieves must give up stealing; rather let them labor and work honestly with their own hands, so as to have something to share with the needy.*

Need I give you another example? Hopefully, you are beginning to see the pattern. Changing behavior is possible, but it requires honestly assessing yourself, resisting temptation and, more importantly, living the answer during times when you aren't tempted.

So, let's say that you are a thief and all you do is tell yourself that you are not going to steal when tempted. If that is all you do, you are not only deceiving yourself, but you are dead on arrival. What goes on between temptations determines what you will do in them.

Most Christians relax when a crisis has passed, instead of using that time to take steps to establish safeguards and get stronger. A thief must keep his grip on a shovel and keep digging even when his compulsion to steal relaxes its grip on him. If he doesn't, he's not serious.

It's also important for a thief to be as sneaky giving away his money as He was pilfering it. Intentionality!! How many times do I need to say this! There is no magic dust for entrenched behavior.

> [29] *Let no evil talk come out of your mouths, but only what is useful for building up, as there is need, so that your words may give grace to those who hear.*

Let me highlight one more. On the surface, this might not seem to have the impact lying and stealing does, but it might have even more. Words that pour out of you unfiltered are like the waste of a steel mill being dumped into a river.

If your words aren't filtered, its pollution will have long-lasting, far-reaching and deleterious effects on the ecosystem. Disease, deformity, the inability to reproduce and even death can result. Glibness, negativity, sarcasm, skepticism, being opinionated, like chemical waste, are the natural byproducts of your attempts to make something out of life in your own strength.

I need to come back to what I told you at the start. You live in two places at the same time. Each have a different language. The language you speak shows where you are most comfortable living. Until you speak heaven's language effortlessly, don't let your words flow unchecked. Filter them!!!

Take inventory of what you say. Like braces, fit God's word into your mouth. At first, you will be painfully aware of how awkward it feels. But when spiritual words become natural, you will become fresh water, refreshing everyone you meet, and healing waters will flow.

> [30] *And do not grieve the Holy Spirit of God, with which you were marked with a seal for the day of redemption.*

These specifics should be enough to get you going in the right direction; but let me tell you why these are so important. Living in default mode does not make the Spirit happy. The Holy Spirit is so aware of the true delight of heaven that when He encounters self-centered behavior that hurts and divides, it pains Him.

The Spirit is such a gentle soul. Dealing with squabbles is not His forte'. Other than wooing, encouraging and warning, there is not much He can do. Since He does not exert His will on His friends, He often is at a loss for words and wants to leave.

Until you begin to act contrary to your old nature, you will only be aware of your own feelings and point of view and won't be able to feel His. On top of that, you will even find it difficult to believe that God feels at all.

But oh, the freedom you will sense when your instincts and actions are in sync with God's Spirit! What joy! And as these moments stretch into days, your sense of worth will grow until that Day when all will see the reason Jesus shed His blood for you.

CHAPTER 4

> [31] *Put away from you all bitterness and wrath and anger and wrangling and slander, together with all malice,*

So, stop the bickering! Stop the fighting! And cut the attitude. You can take your ball and go home Him if you want; but if you do, don't expect the Spirit to go with you. He is not into solo.

The reason your life is filled with people is so you can learn to play together. But you react to this. You fume over that. You still get stupid over silly stuff. If you continue down this path, your little attitude and sniping will detonate and who knows what irreparable damage will be done?

> [32] *and be kind to one another, tenderhearted, forgiving one another, as God in Christ has forgiven you.*

Rather, act kindly toward each other whether you feel like it or not. You must choose to act like God to become the person God imagined you to be. And with all the sorts of people who invade your life, you will have plenty of opportunity to be kind. And when you do, you will discover that this is a near impossible task.

It wasn't any easier for Christ. In fact, take your difficulty and multiply that to the nth degree. Don't think that Jesus wasn't affected by the misunderstandings, the insults and abuse, and the rejection. It wasn't a walk in the park for Him either. He even sweated blood.

Jesus learned to lean completely upon His Father to do in Him those things He found difficult to do naturally. On the cross, in the face of all the savagery directed toward Him, He discovered His Father in Him being kind, so He was. He felt His Father forgiving, so He forgave.

The Father has always been forgiving. He has always been kind. His heart has always yearned for humanity. But on the cross, in that single moment of time, when all of our grotesque ugliness came out of the shadows, the Father could, at last, tangibly and perfectly express all of His feelings toward humanity through His Son. And Christ let Him.

There are moments when the Father desires to extend His kindness toward those around you. These are the times are when you too are crossed. If you are not aware of this, you will let the devil enact his vengeance on others through you, rather than have them taste God's goodness.

Why do you think He put His life in you and put others in your life? The Father still is forgiving. He still is kind. His heart still yearns to embrace each and every one. Only now He expresses Himself through you. So, let Him.

CHAPTER 5

> [1] *Therefore be imitators of God, as beloved children,* [2] *and live in love, as Christ loved us and gave himself up for us, a fragrant offering and sacrifice to God.*

I know, however, that it was different for Jesus. He neither had a propensity for evil, nor did he have to deal with entrenched behaviors and their scarring effects. Jesus has ever been in the embrace of His Father and has desired nothing else.

Yours is a more difficult task because someone who was obese will still think of himself as fat even though he's lost a bunch of weight. And a poor person's perception of himself won't change just because he wins the lottery.

So, it makes perfect sense that even though you have been adopted by God and loved in every way, you still struggle with your identity and find it hard to let your guard down. And your behavior shows it. These fears will never allow you to love like He does.

The only self that Jesus knows is bathed in Father's attention and affection, so love is His second nature. But you will need, in both good times and bad, in your back-slidings and front-slidings, again and again, to reassure your own heart of God's love before these false perceptions of yourself will fade.

But just reordering your thought life is not enough to change how you see yourself. You must act lovingly towards others around you in order to cement your identity in Christ because your perception of your self is reinforced by your actions. Have you noticed that when you don't feel welcome and you pull back, the feeling of not being welcome grows? But if you reach out then, these feelings recede.

It is a well-established principle that feelings and perceptions, both positive and negative, follow your actions whether you are trusting Jesus or not. But being God-like and loving like God requires more than you trying to love because His love is rooted in Himself and not in you.

Loving like Christ will bring you to the end of yourself because loving like Him is impossible for you. Only Jesus can love this type of love, and only Jesus in you can. And since He went through the process of death, burial and resurrection, don't expect anything different. Dying to yourself to find Christ's life alive in you will be painful as well.

Jesus kept Himself in His Father's love when it seemed like no one else cared. You too will need to learn how to do this when life turns its ugly side toward you. When others hate, Jesus loves you and, in you, loves. As you begin to let Jesus love others through you, your sense of being loved will increase and it will become easier for you to love others which will then increase your awareness of being God's child. What a glorious cycle!

Look at Jesus. The depth of the love He experienced from His Father matched the love He gave. And it staggers me to think about the sort of love He knew when His last breath was exhaled on the cross.

As the awareness of His affection grows in you, you will begin seeing others in the same light. And in moments of their ugliness, instead of reacting or retreating, you too will open your arms with no other agenda but to extend God's love.

> [3] *But fornication and impurity of any kind, or greed, must not even be mentioned among you, as is proper among saints.* [4] *Entirely out of place is obscene, silly, and vulgar talk; but instead, let there be thanksgiving.*

Let me now talk about love by contrasting it to what it ain't. What it isn't is playing in mud holes. If you choose the mud, you

CHAPTER 5

will continue to look for love and significance in all the wrong places. Mud holes might be ok for small children, but if you keep frequenting them, your name will be mud and you won't want to show your face.

As I have said before, you came into His family with strong emotional attachments to things you thought would satisfy. But continuing to consume these things will only make you smaller and emptier and needier. Drinking saltwater to quench your thirst is a futile endeavor.

I am specifically talking about your strong desire toward all things sexual and the more subtle, yet equally destructive, propensity to fill your internal, sacred spaces with things. Of all the many things that can take hold of you, these grip tightest in their attempt to enslave you.

Have you pulled back the layers to see what is driving this? Acting out sexually tells me that you were made for intimacy. And consuming things (whether food or the latest toy) to fill a void in your life, tells me that you were made to be full and overflowing.

You need such an aversion to the devil's substitutes that when these are brought up in conversation, the hairs on the back of your neck will stand up. Know that whatever fills your life, consumes it.

The issue is not that behavior just reflects the person you believe yourself to be, it also strengthens that identity. And, with some of you, these behaviors are still automatic and define you! Don't let them do that because this is not who you are!!!

And if you are not sure what you believe about yourself, listen to what comes out of your mouth. Your words will betray what you really believe about yourself and about God every time. And I am not just talking about the obvious words, like "poor me" or "damn it."

Funny words are just as bad. While expletives might be more direct, jesting, as self-deprecating as it might be, also deflects from the real issue which is a false image of yourself. If your first response is anything but thanks and praise, you haven't got it yet.

That is why you need to be over the top in giving thanks because I have found that thanksgiving is not only God's antidote to everything pernicious; but it is also the true measure of humility. Expressing thanks to God each and every day for each and every thing brings your life into perspective. "Thanks" acknowledges His sovereignty and goodness, while reminding you of who you are—a gift, full of God's favor.

And though this might seem forced at times, giving thanks is entirely in character with the you God created and will slowly chip away at the facade that you have. If your words aren't filled with thanks, the very words that pour out of your mouth will make you more and more comfortable with living in the slop-hole God has pulled you from.

> [5] *Be sure of this, that no fornicator or impure person, or one who is greedy (that is, an idolater), has any inheritance in the kingdom of Christ and of God.*

Now I am going to say some things which might seem, at face value, said only for shock value. And you might even accuse me of not being as grace-filled as I say I am. But God's grace is as costly as it is free.

Please pay attention, this is far more serious than you can imagine. If you don't take it seriously, you will lose out big time even though God has already given to you all that He is and has. And you needn't look any further than my people's history to know that this is true.

Israel was promised so much more than they obtained, and even lost possession of what God had given to them. Like Israel, you have enemies both within and without who would keep you from taking and enjoying what God has promised. In a bit, I will talk with you about the "enemy without"; but until you face down the "enemy within," your inheritance is at risk and the "enemy without" needn't bother with you at all.

While Israel's inheritance consisted of a physical geography, yours is spiritual, and is determined by the extent you possess your own soul. Israel was first to conquer the nations which inhabited and acculturated the land before they could possess and cultivate what God had set apart for Himself.

You too must deal decisively with your entrenched behaviors and not just see them as forgivable weaknesses that you have no control over. Israel was greatly affected by those they allowed to

CHAPTER 5

coexist with them. Little by little they lost their distinctiveness and instead of becoming, in heart and soul, the people of God, they became His enemy. Don't let that happen to you.

As long as you coexist with your sexual predilections, you are in danger of becoming a pervert regardless of how graced you are. And if you don't deal decisively with your greed, it will consume you. You will not only worship at its altar of dust, but will become as inconsequential as dust.

> [6] *Let no one deceive you with empty words, for because of these things the wrath of God comes on those who are disobedient.* [7] *Therefore do not be associated with them.*

Don't be fooled, God has a vindictive side and His anger might burn hot against you. Now I really don't want to talk about the angry side of God. His anger is reserved, anyway, for the devil and his offspring—those who declare their ignorance to be truth, regardless of the facts, and then, like the devil, resist Him at every turn.

But if God's generosity doesn't win you over, He does have a jealous side. He has too much invested to be apathetic and let you slide. The worst thing He can do anyway is to throw up His hands and leave you to your own devices.

If you persist though, He just might do it. He did with Israel. Until that point, however, He will use both the carrot and the stick to keep you from creating safe spaces for His enemy to inhabit, even if it means getting a little hot under the collar.

So be careful who you listen to. Talkers talk and can say some fairly convincing things. You need to develop an ear for God and train your heart to obey Him. Only then, will you be able to discern His voice in others.

You are totally responsible for your life and what you allow to influence you. You cannot claim that you were deceived because deception is a fruit of your own laziness and desires. God does not hide Himself from those who deeply desire Him and seek truth.

So, beware of those who minimize your behavior by talking only about God's acceptance and forgiveness without the need to learn bare-knuckle fighting. This also applies to those who minimize God's extravagant grace by trying to guilt you into a relationship with the God who loves unconditionally. Both are setting you up for failure. If you buy into either, you will have no one to blame but yourself. So don't do it!

> [8] *For once you were darkness, but now in the Lord you are light. Live as children of light—* [9] *for the fruit of the light is found in all that is good and right and true.* [10] *Try to find out what is pleasing to the Lord.*

Let me take a step back for a moment and talk about principles because I don't have time to mention all the behaviors that choke the Life out of you. I've only mentioned the biggies. You really don't want me continually to harrumph about this or about that, do you?

And since I want to turn my attention to behaviors that accelerate Life and embody love, I won't have time to enumerate all of those either. So, let me lay out a principle to help you navigate the gray areas of your soul.

Besides if you want to be a growing child of God, you must be done with rule-keeping anyway. I want you to have a template so you can figure this out for yourself and determine what delights God. This principle has been evident from the beginning. And as you become aware of it, you will see it played out again and again in Scriptures and, more and more, in you. The principle is this: Darkness consumes, and Light emanates.

In the beginning, before the light exposed the darkness for what is was, darkness shrouded the earth, God's desired dwelling. It was a felt darkness—a darkness that hid all potentiality and everything beautiful.

This darkness stripped value from everything it touched and left whatever it swirled around, empty. It resisted all that was good and choked out all Life. Under its cloud, darkness dragged everything further into its abyss. Darkness is anything but passive.

The same darkness which shrouded the earth, both covered and perfectly described you. You were a black hole consuming and being consumed, all the while being controlled by the prince of darkness. As such, you sought to control your own universe because darkness, by nature, is controlling and self-seeking, self-absorbing, self-pleasuring and self-centered.

CHAPTER 5

But a radical change has occurred. You are now not just enlightened, but you are light—diametrically opposed to all that you once were. Your nature is to shine like Him and to radiate without regard for self, not using things or people to meet your own needs.

Understanding this dichotomy will allow you to distinguish between darkening behaviors and light-filled actions. And as you move into the light, you will discover the effects of being light-saturated—the first being, seeing God as He is.

For all eternity, the Father, Son and Spirit have oozed with goodness toward each other, and then toward all things created. This is so indescribably unlike anything that you have experienced that it is hard to believe at first or second or even third blush. But as you encounter the God who is good in all the vicissitudes of life, you will open wide your heart to Him.

And as you see Him more clearly, you will also see yourself in the same light. The shadows that have darkened your perceptions of self will be dispersed by the realization that you are included in and the object of this eternal overflow.

Shame will give way to glory. No more thinking less of yourself. No more, "I am nots!" No more, "'If' I am the son of God." If? If? Indeed! You are a son of God! That didn't work on Jesus and shouldn't work on you.

For you are, as Christ is, righteous–inextricably entwined in the interplay of God and enveloped in His goodness. You are no longer caught up in rule-keeping, but in the relationship of relationships because the light has revealed Him, and you in Him and Him in you.

These two things together, His goodness and your righteousness, is the truth that sets free. For as you see both Him and your self in this light, you will have a new framework to interpret life. And as you grapple with these new concepts, you will discover heaven seeping in through the cracks of your soul and will hear Him whisper, "You are my beloved child. I am so proud of you."

> [11] *Take no part in the unfruitful works of darkness, but instead expose them.* [12] *For it is shameful even to mention what such people do secretly;*

As this light dawns on you, you will find yourself going a step further because the end game is not for you alone to experience His smile. God wants everyone to sense His favor.

Those who live in darkness are unaware of His yearning for them since the same shame that blinded Adam blinds them. And their actions and reactions further block this light from shining. Instead of living free and anticipating more and more good, they crawl further under the cover of darkness.

This is exactly why God has you hovering around their empty and confused lives. Can't you see, when you look at their faces, that something is so very wrong, deep down?

God looked on the world and did not walk away. No, He brooded over the world like a hen covering her soon-to-be chicks, and in doing so, claimed the mess as His. Then He spoke. Regardless the depth of that darkness, He spoke to uncover the beauty that was hidden.

Do you understand my analogy? God did not rebuke the darkness (though the darkness is rebukable.) He stepped into it by speaking, "Light." He told the world who He was and dispelled the darkness. He spoke what He envisioned, and life took shape. He spoke the answer and questions left.

Each day there are people around you, unaware of their God-kissed beauty who try to dispel this darkness the best they can. Their efforts are fruitless, however, and bring no clarity to who or why they are.

> [13] *but everything exposed by the light becomes visible,* [14] *for everything that becomes visible is light.*

So, speak into their darkness. Let them know the gift that He is to them and the gift they are to Him. Speak of His forgiveness so they will become aware of sin. Speak of their destiny that they might realize their meager existence. Speak of who they are so they can leave their old life behind.

And when they open their heart as you did, they, like you, will find light flooding in and will also become light in the Lord.

> *Therefore it says, "Sleeper, awake! Rise from the dead, and Christ will shine on you."*

CHAPTER 5

Since you are the light that God has determined to shine on others, wake up so He can flood your soul with light. A big reason that others have not been warmed by the Son is that you are still in bed with the covers over your head.

There is no excuse for that. It's time, high time, to get out of your comfort zone. Experiencing God and everything He has called you to is a step or two outside of that zone.

So, get out of bed. I mean, literally, get out of bed. If you need to stomp around the house to engage your soul, do it. If you need to shout to get yourself out of neutral, do it. You have been passive long enough. You are still afraid of your own voice. You are still afraid to be a little foolish before the Lord.

> [15] *Be careful then how you live, not as unwise people but as wise,* [16] *making the most of the time, because the days are evil.*

But don't be foolish when you leave your house. Be mindful of every step you take. You cannot assume success if you meander throughout your day. That is plain stupid.

Know that God has planned each and every day for you, so live each day like He has. Set an alarm to remind yourself to praise Him. At minimum, remember to pray and cry out to Him in the evening, at morning and at noon. He promises to hear your voice. This is how you take your life back!

When you are intentional about your moments, your days will fall in line and your life will be absorbed into the eternity of God. While time will not stand still for you, it can work for you if you learn to structure it. Like gold, it will not benefit you unless you see its worth and do the hard work required to mine it.

And don't put this off because time is not your friend. Don't fall into the trap of either thinking that there is not enough time (so why begin at all?) or that there is more than enough (so why begin now?). You will not have tomorrow if you think it will wait for you. You will only have tomorrow if you think it won't.

> [17]*So do not be foolish but understand what the will of the Lord is.* [18] *Do not get drunk with wine, for that is*

debauchery; but be filled with the Spirit, ("with the Spirit" in Greek is "in the Spirit")

Now that I have your complete attention, let me tell you the secret of getting the God who lives inside of you out for the world to see. For regardless of what I have just laid out (that is, the need to face your entrenched behaviors and the skewed beliefs that feed them), you will never really be free of the negatives of your life just by fighting against them. Like quicksand, the more you struggle against them, the more you are sucked in.

If you understand this, you are a step closer to understanding God's intent for your life, and it is not about focusing on minutia. God's will for you is about being more and more, not about doing this or that. But when the concept of being grabs you, oh the doing you will do!

Have you ever seen someone who is plastered? Is He trying to act like he's drunk? I don't think so. Do you need to smell his breath or test his blood to know that he is? Hardly.

You know because you see how free he is. And it doesn't matter whether he's belligerent or the life of the party, he is himself, unleashed from the inhibitions that have kept the real person hidden. Self-conscious would not be one of his descriptors, neither would "prim and proper."

This is exactly God's plan for you–that you would be so juiced, others would ask, "What's up with you?" But unless you are filled with the same Spirit-brew the Father and Jesus are, you will, in your attempts to "be like Christ" exhaust yourself and annoy others.

The good news is that you have been immersed in same Spirit. Therefore, it should be easier for you to be the person God imagined you be than it is for a drunk, living in a vat of beer, to remain drunk. The difference is that a drunk knows how to drink. That is why my greatest task is to show you how to drink, and to drink often and deeply.

But before I show you how, you need some background in order to understand the importance of drinking the Spirit and knowing where to drink. To do that, I need to take you back to the beginning where Adam and Eve drank of the Spirit in the garden.

CHAPTER 5

Though they were probably unaware of what they were doing, you need to know so you can be intentional.

From one source, four rivers flowed from Eden. From these rivers, Adam and Eve drank and refreshed themselves. On these rivers, they and their descendants were also to extend their reach and take what they learned in Eden to subjugate a hostile world. And as they established God's kingdom throughout the world, these rivers would sustain them.

Adam and Eve also lived in four different relationships from which they drank and refreshed themselves. These relationships affirmed and instructed them about who they were, about life and their destiny. These relationships were firstly with their own self, then their relationship with God, then their relationship with each other and lastly with their environment. Before these rivers were poisoned, these relationships witnessed to them that they were right, and so they drank deeply.

They sensed God's "yes" in the cool of the day, every day. Their conscience also said "yes" in all they did. Their spouse said yes as well, confirming each other's worth and calling. And their environment did not resist them at all.

After they fell, they kept drinking from these rivers but instead of being confirmed, they were condemned. These rivers, now poisoned, produced the brokenness, the heartache and the death mankind has experienced ever since.

The first stream was their perception of self. Instead of living in an unconscious awareness of their own beauty and perfection, shame covered their ugliness. For the first time, Adam knew something against himself and from that time on, mankind has covered himself with anything he could to make himself look good.

And then, even though God's heart for them did not change in any way, their heart toward Him did, as did their perception of Him. No longer perceived as good, Adam and Eve kept away as far as possible from God. His closeness was no longer desired because His presence became a threat in their mind. The God-stream became poisoned as well and, from that, we also drank.

And since Adam and Eve became self-serving, their relationship with each other became toxic. Instead of caring for each other, they began using each other for their own ends and to meet their own needs. Instead of extending a beckoning hand, they began pointing an accusing finger which still points today.

Lastly, their environment began to affect them adversely. Instead of fruit, thorns sprung up. Life turned its prickly side toward them and began to resist them at every turn. Circumstances which once clapped for them began to slap them, as they still do for many.

Fear and uncertainty replaced a confident assurance in life and this four-fold death made them smaller and smaller until they perished. The righteous, who knew they were right, became uncertain and un-right about everything and as a result, developed their own self-righteousness..

Each of these four spheres, which were designed to satisfy, ruptured and disintegrated in the fall and became areas of great conflict. Therefore God needed, on the cross, not to only redeem you, but also to clean up these four rivers from which you drink.

These springs are now bubbling up in you into eternal life. These rivers, which were once death, are now the refreshing and restorative rivers of the Spirit. But unless you aware of this and learn how to drink, being "filled in the Spirit" will remain a foreign concept, and rather than flowing, the boulders in you will keep you stagnant and block the flow of life. And instead of tasting sweetness in these relationships, they will still taste bitter.

> [19] *as you sing psalms and hymns and spiritual songs among yourselves, (in Greek, speaking to yourselves with psalms, hymns, and songs from the spirit.)*

So, let me help with the drinking part. The first river redeemed is you, and how important it is for you to know this. Unless you persuade yourself that you are God-imagined and God-kissed, the real you will continue to hide. You will not be able to encourage your brothers and sisters, let alone affect the world, until you know personally the you God imagined.

I wish that this could happen automatically by going to church or small group. Listening to your pastor will not do it, neither will meeting in small group. This will only work if the truth that you hear from others becomes the truth you say to yourself.

CHAPTER 5

You are the most influential person in your life. You are the best preacher you will ever hear and the best audience you will ever preach to. So, what have you been telling yourself? Anything? What do you hear being played on your internal digital recorder?

The junk you've recorded about yourself from your earliest years can be overwritten, but only you can do it. You have been given a mouth, so use it and speak to yourself! David did. The psalms he wrote for himself are for your use as well. Engage your own soul and breathe courage into yourself. Learn the secret of David's, "Ohh!"

The secret is out. In the realm of the Spirit, drinking is speaking, and speaking is drinking. So, speak extravagant things about yourself, to yourself. You cannot out-extravagant God! What He has said about you is far more wonderful and heretical than you can ever say.

Don't you know that when He glimpses you, His breath is taken away? So, use your breath to blow away the death-dust that layers your soul by speaking His love for you, outload.

Do these thoughts make you uncomfortable? If so, you have not yet discovered the beauty that is you or the love that is God's. Do you think that agape love is dispassionate and distant? It isn't.

This God is so over the top with you. While it is right to worship the God who sits on His throne, have you ever worshipped the God who adores you? God is overcome by the thought of you. He obsesses over you and stalks you.

Your perception of God's love is too platonic. God's love is not a "have to" love and goes way beyond a "want to" love. His passion for you overpowers Him, and for you to think anything less is faulty thinking and false humility.

So, put down your theology and discipleship books and start reading Harlequin novels. There is a reason Harlequin novels outsell all other genres. They deeply resonate because they reveal the deep longing in your deepest part for the affection and attention of Another. You were wired for a love like this and God wants you to start seeing yourself as His love interest.

singing and making melody to the Lord in your hearts,

You might ask why I prioritize addressing yourself before worshipping and ministering to God. It's simple. Unless you embrace the you, with a small "y," God created and see yourself as an equal, with a small "e," your attempts to connect with God will fall short of what He desires.

God created you for relationship, but not a relationship between dis-similars, like you and your dog, for example. No matter how comforting and entertaining you might find Fido, he will never get your jokes. Satisfying relationships blend hearts together who have a common heritage and a shared life. God is so over the mentality which says that you less than a friend or a son or a lover.

Have you ever sung a duet with your dog? You can certainly howl with him, but he can never harmonize with you. You must be able to look into each other's eyes to blend your voices together and follow each other's lead. Only equals can do that. Only those who sense that the other would add to their song are willing to share the stage. Only the ones who can give equal worth to the other will open their hearts and mouths wide because blending one's soul exposes you to risk like little else.

And harmonize you must. Take stock of what happens in your mind and heart when you spend time with Him. With many, quiet times are just that—quiet. Because of this, times in His presence can be scattered. If your mind is blank, write on it. If it is empty, fill it. And I can think of nothing better than to fill it with song.

You see, heaven is filled with music and not because creation is singing. It is song-filled because the Lord, with His beer stein, leads the chorus just like the linen-ed David led his cohorts in celebration.

God pre-existed the heavens and from eternity has played all sorts of music. Creation sings counterpoint. And when He made His home within you, He brought His music along with Him. The Trio came with the guitar and the bass and drums. He is looking to you for the vocals. So like David, let your tongue be the pen of the skillful Scribe.

Take David's words as your starting point and sing them from your heart back to the Lord. Then add to David's words, your own

CHAPTER 5

postscripts. You will be amazed, at times, the connection you will sense.

Since faith both acts on spiritual realities and makes real to you what is real in Him, stop the inner silence and begin, at the very least, to hum. Take out your heart, the best instrument ever created, and ask Him to tune it to His. Harmonizing with Him will not only connect you with heaven, but also will bring heaven to earth.

> [20] *giving thanks to God the Father at all times and for everything in the name of our Lord Jesus Christ.*

Now that I have addressed the internals, let me turn my attention to the externals. Ministering both to yourself and to God gives you the strength to deal with the circumstances and people that can drain you. Unless you find fullness within, forget about navigating life without. If you find life overwhelming and people annoying, go back to step one. Your reactions to life are the best way to determine where you are in the process and where to place your attention.

Your circumstances are the scenes in which God writes your story. And your story is His story being played out once again. Yours is the story of Abraham, growing in faith. Yours is the story of David—a nobody becoming a somebody. Yours is the story of Ruth—an outsider becoming an insider. Ultimately yours is the story of Jesus because as He is, so are you in the world. Your circumstances push and pull, stretch and compress, and hinder and propel you toward your place in God's ever-expanding story of redemption.

God uses each circumstance to carry you toward your destiny even when it seems like the currents are stagnant or even taking you in an opposite direction. Without knowing this, you could find yourself rowing hard against the Spirit's work in your life.

A simple test is this: listen to what comes or does not come out of your mouth when life happens. Silence often is unbelief because it hides "I can't believe this is happening to me" by putting on a good front. Cursing removes all doubts as to whether you believe in the sovereign goodness, purpose and power of God. Thanksgiving is the only appropriate response because your circumstances are no longer against you. Those thorns have flowered.

As the Father repurposed Jesus' cross and made that seeming end a beginning, He has already repurposed yours. Every single thing that has happened in your past and every single thing to occur in your future has already been redeemed. Each circumstance is an open door into more of God and into a greater unveiling of you. And to live in this fullness, you must add your amen to life as it occurs.

At times, giving thanks will seem forced; but when it does, be forceful because it leads to a life of effortless thankfulness. You will begin seeing life and what it brings as a hand-picked gift from your loving Father that comes to bless your life. Responding to life with thanks will transform your life because this simple act cements God's grace in your heart, makes you a joy to be around and discombobulates the devil. The devil does not know what to do with "thank you."

[21] *Be subject to one another out of reverence for Christ.*

I hope you are beginning to understand that being "filled with the spirit" is as practical as it is spiritual. When you look back on your life, you will thank me for blurring the spiritual/practical lines because there is no difference. Spiritual realities require the tangible stuff of life to become real to you.

Speaking to yourself might not seem that spiritual. Neither does keeping a song in your heart. And it might seem that taking your soul in hand and rehearsing God's goodness to it in times of trouble is a whole lot of you and not so much Spirit, but, if that is the case, your vision is still fuzzy.

The reason I am taking time to talk through these things is because I know how difficult it is to fit these thoughts together. But I also know that if you continue to walk out the practical steps I am laying out before you, Jesus still turns water into wine, that is, the natural will become spiritual. You are aware, aren't you, that wine is still 85% water? Do you catch my drift?

Now there is one last area I need to address concerning redemption and fullness and practicalities and drinking. I am going to need even more time to talk about this, not because this sphere

CHAPTER 5

of redemption is more important than the previous three, but this is where the other three are played out.

In fact, this is where heaven and hell, light and darkness collide. It is the place of your greatest pain and greatest joy. It is where your defense mechanisms are on high alert and where you need the most help. I am talking about your day-in, day-out relationships.

Like the cross, these relationships expose you in a way nothing else can. Your inner person is on display for all to see. Initially, what you see will not be pretty because relationships are God's chosen tool to expose and magnify your brokenness. And when you throw another broken person into the mix, these interactions can increase your exposure exponentially. Relationships reveal how truly self-centered you are.

Irritation, impatience, anger, stubbornness, argumentativeness, the need to get your own way and be right, to get the last word, sulking and the like are all revealed in relationship. This is a good thing because you will know the "before" of God's redemptive power and be able to testify to the "after." The good news of God always begins with bad news about yourself which is really good news.

Relationships are also the most efficient way to bring about change in your life. Like the cross, they are God's instrument to transform you. And like the cross, it is a painful place where you are hung out to dry and die, if you choose not to escape as many do. You need to hang in there long enough before you can expect yourself or your relationship to change. Death always precedes resurrection. Always.

So, earn a PhD on the significant others in your life. You will only receive this degree through much prayer, and through trial and error. And then from your heart, adapt to them in such a way that you lift them up and fill their empty spaces. In doing so, you will find freedom for yourself and they will find healing.

In a word, submit to them. Submission has received such bad press because of shallow thinking. I can only imagine what comes to your mind when you hear this word. They are almost fighting words. "Submit to whom!?" "To him?" "To her?" "Yea, right. I don't think so."

EPHESIANS AND ALL THAT JAZZ

But I hope you realize that the Submitter in Chief does not see it this way. Not one bit! In fact, I am invoking His name again because it is Jesus' nature to "wash feet," whether it is His Father's or yours. He gets off His throne so effortlessly every time someone interrupts. And it's time to get off yours.

And I am also bringing up His name because you might think that the person interrupting your life is Joe or Jane or Mike. It's not. It's Jesus. You are meeting Him every time you encounter friends or strangers. That is why I am not put off by the peculiarities of others or their interruptions. I am not going to roll my eyes at Jesus. Besides the only way to a healthier self-esteem is to lower yourself and serve others.

Of all the ways the Lord could have chosen to win your affection and allegiance, adapting to you was the method He chose. Submitting was His way to change the likes of you and me, and still is. What elegant subtlety, submission is. What subterfuge!

On the surface, you would think that being told that you are His central focus and that He has committed Himself to meeting all your needs would strengthen the selfish part of you. But this has the exact opposite effect. Jesus' serving you frees you to serve Him and all those made in His image.

And as speaking God's word to yourself is the best way to connect with the you God made, and creating a symphony within is the best way to attract an audience with God, and as giving thanks is the best way to get your circumstances to work for you and not against you, getting underneath someone else is the absolute best way to find your worth.

> [22] *Wives, be subject to your husbands as you are to the Lord.*

Now knowing your penchant for nodding and not really hearing, let me look you in the eyes and talk directly to you about the relationships which matter most in your life. And be aware that I am both an equal opportunity offender and encourager. You might think I am picking on you by talking about your role, but what I am really doing is helping you see your great worth.

CHAPTER 5

If I am right that adapting yourself to others will set you free and give you tremendous influence in their lives, then don't take what I am about to say and ask, "what about him or her?" One of the best ways to neutralize God's power is to read someone else's playbook to remind them of their part while overlooking yours. No, read from your own playbook and do your part.

The specific relationships I am going to discuss are two parts of a whole and most reflect the Godhead. As such, these relationships also are the primary focus of the devil's attack. These roles are wives and husbands, dads and children, and employer and employees.

I will first begin with you wives because you are the key to making this work. Men are often clueless and need help getting it. Yes, they are initiators, but often lack direction. God has given you a greater sensitivity and many times, like Mary at the tomb, get the revelation first. Because the male species is obtuse, God brought you together.

Your husband might pigeon-hole you, assuming what role you play in your relationship. Adam did. He named his wife, "Eve," which means "the mother of all who live." He defined her role and relegated her to motherhood while he did his own thing. While I don't disagree with his estimation, he might have been a bit self-serving.

God thinks about you differently, and you must accept His valuation first. While Adam called his wife "Eve" after the fall, God named her "Ezer" before the fall. God named her, and by extension you, with the same name He calls Himself—Helper. To be more precise, "Helper right in front of him." (Genesis 2:18)

Ladies, God has put you right in front of him to help the boy. God wanted a personal representative in front of the man every day because men tend to go hell-bent chasing whims, and they need the checks and balances you provide.

Remember a helper is always in a greater position than the help-ee, so don't buy into the devil's lies which say you are less. That definition was corrupted in the fall. God called you to be a "helper-like-God" so you would take your rightful place in the relationship.

Let him know that you are there to keep him from falling off the rails. On the matters of little importance, give in. Sex and socks, by the way, are little things. This is where you typically miss the mark. If you choose these areas on which to focus your help, it will be harder for him to listen to you in the areas which matter most.

To gain full access to his heart, act from your heart as if he was your Lord. This might seem like the stuff doormats are made of, but it isn't. It's called strategy. You might think, knowing him as you do, that the only outcome of this plan is to build his ego. It is really to build yours and give you your rightful place as chief influencer.

Love him this way because it is the best way to get through his maze of defenses. Your husband has his guard up all day and sadly doesn't know when to take it down. I know that this will take some time and that you will suffer some of the residual effects of his ego along the way, but you are in good company because the Lord did also.

The goal of this action plan is for you to have the same relationship with your husband as the Lord desires with you. God does not want to relate to someone who is distant or Stepford-ish; but a person who is fully alive, and self-possessed, and as independent a thinker as He is.

The Lord desires that you and He be a team, collaborating as you navigate life. And as you find ways to be His servant, you'll discover that you will become the friend Jesus desires, confides in and listens to. Marriage is intended to work the same way

> [23] *For the husband is the head of the wife just as Christ is the head of the church, the body of which he is the Savior.* [24] *Just as the church is subject to Christ, so also wives ought to be, in everything, to their husbands.*

because your marriage correlates exactly to the church and Christ. You give voice to this as you act out this unseen reality in your home. Every morning, when you get out of bed, you are standing on holy ground. You needn't to go to a convent to encounter Jesus, you just need to open your eyes.

I know what you see is not always pretty because the guy who walks around in his underwear is not as exciting as the one who walked down the aisle. But as you have probably discovered, the Church is like this as well. You need to look past personalities and

CHAPTER 5

your preferences to find Him and your joy in Him, either at church or home.

Dying to your self is the only way to encounter Christ. You trip over yourself every time you shut down or rise up. You still need to be saved from your selfish self; and God often uses the selfish guy next to you in bed to expose your heart in order for Jesus to bring healing and wholeness to you. The Lord, in a round-about way, uses your husband, as unwitting as he is, to save you from yourself.

So, stop expecting him to make the first move in making you feel safe, even though that is his primary job. Make him feel welcome and safe at home by respecting him from your heart just as you would expect the church to do when Jesus shows up. It will be painfully intentional at first; but like every aspect of the Christian life, as you continue to act by faith that he is your beloved and you are his, you will experience Jesus' life alive in you.

[25] *Husbands, love your wives, just as Christ loved the church and gave himself up for her,*

I have the exact same message for you husbands. "Adapt to your wife." But I must take a different tact to get my point across to you since you're not wired like her. Men need to know the rationale upfront along with the plan and what's in it for them in order to get fully engaged. And I am ok with that since I can talk more about Jesus.

Your wife's focus is Christ–responding to His love through all your un-loveliness and submitting to Him in your failings. Your focus also is Christ; but, as men, you are called to take it to a different level. You are to be the initiator, not only acting like Christ toward her, but from deep within, being Christ to her, and not, as I have said, the one who sits on his throne.

He sits because His work is done. Yours isn't. Your wife is still a bundle of worries, and of feelings of not being appreciated or loved or important or safe. These hide beneath the surface waiting to come out. Her nitpicking, by the way, is the best way she has in that moment, to express these "below the surface" feelings. They are not really an attack on you, but a deeply felt heart cry.

And you are not "Jesus before her" if you explode or try to reason or bully her into your point of view, or if you leave in a huff. If you interpret these interactions as either her issue or as an attack on you, it tells me a couple things. You neither know your wife, nor know how God un-messes the messy. How can you cooperate with God and His efforts if you are clueless?

Just like Christ with the Church, you are to win and quiet her heart by giving yourself so completely to the mess you come home to that you become less and less aware of the mess that she is and more and more aware of the beauty she is becoming. I am asking you to love her in such a way that she can, in her times of her perceived ugliness, rest in your love and, in the middle of uncertain times, feel safe.

That is the goal. Now this is the plan. When Jesus committed Himself to His bride, He left His universes behind and gave up every one of his hobbies to make her His world and hobby. With eyes wide open, He plotted how to win over a bride who didn't believe she was beautiful and who rejected her own worth.

This was not an easy process for Jesus and came with great cost. It started with leaving the pleasures of heaven and ended with embracing our pain. And once He stepped into our world, the cost became more apparent, and increased.

The camaraderie of heaven and the familiarity of its surrounds gave way to living with a stranger who spoke a different language and who misinterpreted His intents because she was enmeshed in a different culture. With all those barriers, getting through to her was a bit difficult, to say the least.

Since He knew that words, however kind and gracious, were not enough, He stepped into her world and disrobed little by little until, fully exposed and vulnerable, he took her up in His arms with all her baggage. He demonstrated on the cross, the only love that could possibly win her over—a love for the ugly in her ugliness, for the vicious in her viciousness and for the entrapped in her helplessness.

[26] *in order to make her holy by cleansing her with the washing of water by the word,*

CHAPTER 5

Only this type of love bathes the film that clouds her eyes and keeps her from seeing her beauty in your eyes and His. Only this type of love brings someone unsure of herself out of the shadows to stand without shame in the glare of a spotlight. Only this type of love allows for a true partnership where glory is shared. She, as well as you, were created to share the stage with Him in His glory.

You have a huge part in redeeming your wife. While you are not her savior, you are the one who is to go before and clear the path so she can find Jesus easier. Some of the roadblocks in her path are difficult for her to move and need your muscle. If you don't, you can easily become a major roadblock in her mind, and one of the reasons that she's not aware of her God-kissed beauty or inestimable worth. And that will make your life miserable.

This type of love cannot follow a step by step plan because God's plan is nonlinear, just like your wife. Talk about a match made in heaven! Since the project before you is not a project, but a person, the steps you must follow are the Spirit's steps. And since the Spirit led Jesus first into the wilderness, expect nothing less.

For there in the wilderness, right in the middle of not getting His needs met, Jesus tested what He would soon be proclaiming–that helplessness was the path to influence and power, and that hearing the voice of God sustains. He also confirmed what He already knew, that the devil, not those He came to live with, was the adversary.

God brought you and your wife together so that you would discover this as well for she often is the one used to drive you into the wilderness. So, don't fight that. Retreat into the arms of God before you react or respond.

When you are in the wilderness, use your inability to win her over as the impetus to wrestle with God. Like your wife, you are not yet convinced of His power or His great love for you. Like your wife, you have also used your own efforts to achieve your goals and desires.

As you cry out to God, bury yourself in the Word to find Him. You will discover a verse or thought or promise that strikes you in a different way. When this happens, stop and ask Him to make that real to you. This word might be God's invasion into both your life and your situation because God always sends His word before Him to initiate His work.

Amplify those words by praying them back to God and then by speaking them to yourself and then to her. This little seed houses God's power to enact change. His Word determine your destiny. Your circumstances don't and neither does your wife's accusations. Regardless the turmoil, this word is your reality.

Remember that you live in two different realities, as I said when I opened this letter. Here you have it, her beauty in Christ and what you see around the house. Hold on to His promise, regardless the circumstances. Until Joseph's word came to free him, God's word defined him. This will happen to you as well. It is a painful process, but a needed one. You can only grow in faith when these two realities collide.

These wilderness-discovered, God-spoken words not only sustained Jesus in the wilderness but were the very ones He used to defeat the devil. The manna He meditated on those forty days became the sword He used to neuter the devil. "Man does not only live by natural means, but by every word spoken by God."

Oh, husbands, how I desire for you to hear God's voice for yourself because His voice will not only bring clarity, but will also break your strong, strong will and your need to get your own way! The voice of the Lord shattered the cedars of Lebanon, and it will certainly shatter you as well. And how you need to be broken!

To hear His still, small voice, you need to become still and small. And hearing Him tell you that you are His beloved will allow you to put down your arms and agendas. Only then can you embrace your wife in her moments of ugliness and cause her heart to rest.

> [27] *so as to present the church to himself in splendor, without a spot or wrinkle or anything of the kind—yes, so that she may be holy and without blemish.*

So now let me now tell you what is in it for you. It's the exact same thing that Jesus came for–a beauty who gets more beautiful as the years go by. While Jesus' task spans millennia and countless

CHAPTER 5

saints, you have your wife. What Jesus does in macro, you are to do in micro.

Look at Jesus' prize. He is gaining a partner, a lover, a confidante and a friend to work and play with. As the ages come and go, His bride will ever be at His side, distracting, encouraging and helping Him and as they create universes together.

Adapting to your wife and caring for what she cares for is the best investment you can make here. Your work and portfolio are nothing. Your kids, with all their importance, are secondary. Besides, the best way to love your kids is to love your wife.

If you devote yourself to your wife as Jesus has to the mess you are, you will put yourself in the best position to have, in time, a wife who constantly glows and looks twenty years younger than she is.

> [28] *In the same way, husbands should love their wives as they do their own bodies. He who loves his wife loves himself.* [29] *For no one ever hates his own body, but he nourishes and tenderly cares for it, just as Christ does for the church,*

Let me paint another picture for you that you might understand. Have you ever purposefully thwacked your thumb? I don't think so. But that is exactly what you are doing when you put the hammer down on your wife. You are bloodying your own thumb. You might not realize this because you aren't the one feeling the impact, nor do you yet understand the ramifications of being "joined together."

In life, your activities are centered on avoiding pain and achieving pleasure. I am not just talking about sex, but that proves my point. For example, you experience in your body the pleasure of being acknowledged for a task well done or the release of endorphins when you catch your second wind. You choose your activities around those things that maximize pleasure and minimize pain.

This is what I am talking about when it comes to your wife. Even though your wife is not you, you need to see her that way. You need to have an inner dialogue with yourself before you dialogue with her. Will what you say or do going to frustrate or encourage her? If it will hurt, be a man and restrain yourself. You would restrain someone else from attacking your wife. Why don't you restrain yourself?

And more than that, be proactive. You plan your projects and pre-think your Saturdays around your favorite sports team. You also make sure that you don't miss a meal. This is exactly how you need to look at your wife because that's how Jesus sees and anticipates you because you are part of His body. Now Jesus can do this because, unlike you, He has a perfect faith vision and sees how inextricably entwined you are with Him.

[30] *because we are members of his body.*

But Jesus' faith is not the only thing that instructs Him. He actually saw how this played out with His own eyes once before because He was there when the woman, like taffy, was pulled out of the man. He saw that the two were one before Adam slept and knew they were still one, after. Oneness just looked and felt different, and a whole lot more interesting.

Jesus took notes when they gazed into each other's eyes for the first time. He knew they connected by the look in their eyes because it was the same feeling He had gazing into His Father's. In their encounter, the man and woman knew they had come home because in the other, each sensed a place so familiar and comfortable, and so attractive.

It was a place they could rest and explore. And in the presence of the other, they sensed no threat regardless their differences. In fact, their differences were what excited them. And how could they not feel this way? At their deepest level, in their essence, they were joined.

Now apart, they saw the reflective part of their self, standing there. And It wasn't only that Adam discovered in Eve a soul mate and a sense of community. Adam, in Eve, finally discovered himself because he exclaimed, "At last!!!! Bone of my bone and flesh of my flesh! Me in her; and she, a living mirror!"

You can only get to know yourself in community. You can gain some insight from a book, but flesh to flesh interactions bring the "at last!" knowledge. Contemplating your belly, considering the

CHAPTER 5

vastness of the heavens or even the closeness of God only brings you so far.

The woman who is your wife can bring you home and keep you there. Your common threads will hold you together while your differences will draw you deeper in. Commonness is comfortable but can get old. Differences will throw you off-balance at first, but in the long run, they will keep you intrigued and allow for exploration.

And when what you are exploring is as vast and nuanced as another's heart, you will never get bored. No wonder Adam broke out in song and danced a jig when he saw her! The greatest adventure in the world was standing before Adam; and yours is lying in bed with you. This, by the way, is how Jesus feels about you.

> [31] *"For this reason a man will leave his father and mother and be joined to his wife, and the two will become one flesh."*

No wonder God used this occasion to give instruction to every man who followed to forsake everything in order to pursue this relationship. The Lord desires everyone to know the key to joy beyond their wildest dreams. He knew that the woman came with a new paradigm for living and, going forward, would alter the man's life and priorities forever.

These instructions tell you to take yourself in hand and say, "Self, prioritize the woman you married by leaving all other attachments so you can fit yourself into the puzzle of her life." In doing so, a miracle will happen, and you will find the wholeness that you have been looking for.

And through the ages, this mantra has echoed off of every altar before which countless couples have stood and is recounted in every Godly counseling session where a husband and wife sit. "Leave all and be glued to each other!"

Even the idyll of paradise and God's immediate presence found competition with the allure of the woman. As God would have it, the closeness of Adam's wife began to rival Adam's closeness with God. For while Adam walked with God, he skipped with his wife. While he shared his thoughts with his Friend, he shared his bed with her.

More and more, Adam retreated with the woman to collaborate and play. And how this delighted God. God even commanded Adam to leave their relationship to pursue His wife. Who do you think Adam's father and mother were anyway?

Leaving other relationships with people and things in order to nurture your marriage is neither leaving nor unhealthy. In fact, existing familial relationships mature and grow when you and your wife flourish together. In Godly leavings, there is neither a sense of betrayal nor competition, but a growing family.

But here's the rub. As Adam was soon to find out, marriage became a tangled mess. From childhood, your past has been littered with slights and hurts, unresolved conflicts and false perceptions about yourself which has trapped you in their web. Because of this, your "I do" at the altar was accompanied with so many don'ts and cant's and won'ts. These wait, at a moment's notice, to be dumped out before your spouse.

This gives even more importance to God's instructions because these slights and hurts have a barb which attaches to your soul and keeps you from real intimacy. Every unresolved conflict from your past is a script which plays itself out again and again in your marriage and in your life.

Just because you no longer live with your folks, don't think the anger and disappointment that you had with your dad or the lack of one hasn't come along for the ride. Too often the battles you fight in the present are not with your spouse, but with the phantoms of your past. The phantoms of the past are always played out in real time.

And you are guaranteed to lose unless you recognize this and pack their bags. For to live well you must leave well. Unresolved conflicts with dad or mom, or brother or sister will be the unresolved conflicts with your spouse. This will keep you from flowing together.

As much as you are able, resolve these conflicts because flowing together is God's plan for you and your wife, that is, being as joined emotionally and spiritually as you are physically in bed. Two, yet one–each penetrating the other's soul and spirit and impregnating each other with life. Oil and water may share the same jar, but they cannot co-mingle.

CHAPTER 5

As you detach yourself from everything that holds you to your past and cling to your spouse who is your future, you can and will become one in every way through God's transforming power.

> [32] *This is a great mystery, and I am applying it to Christ and the church.*

God especially focuses His attention on your marriage because it is the microcosm of everything God is about and doing. Your marriage is a fuzzy prophetic picture of Jesus and His bride, the Church. Wow! There are so many layers to this that when I begin to pull them back, it blows my mind and messes with my theology.

Does this mean Christ will soon leave the embrace of His Father to live His life with another? The Scriptures say that a man should leave his father and mother to form another relationship which, in turn, becomes a separate and new entity. Since Scriptures cannot be broken, it sure seems that way to me.

Will the Triune become two Duads? What sort of relationship will the Father and Son have going forward? And who is the Holy Spirit going hang out with now that His best friend is taking a bride? Is the Father going to give the bride away and invoke the blessing?

So many questions, but I cannot go there right now. But I feel in my bones that this thing we take for granted and often give up on, this much maligned relationship called marriage, is the seed of eternities to come.

> [33] *Each of you, however, should love his wife as himself, and a wife should respect her husband.*

You can see how easily I can get off track. Sorry. I know these thoughts are for another time and place, so let me get back to focusing on what's before us because that is all we can control.

Men, in short, do yourself a favor and favor your wife. In fact, you can bring yourself into more and more of God's favor by putting the preferences of your wife before your own. And dear women, show genuine interest in what interests your husband. Learn to draw him out and listen. These simple things will affect eternity.

CHAPTER 6

¹Children, obey your parents in the Lord, for this is right.

Kids, just because you are young and small does not mean that I am going to change my message for you. You need to learn to submit as well; but submitting for you will look a little different than it does for your folks. Your mom and dad submit to each other as equals, but that's not how it is for you. Your folks are the boss of you, and you are to obey them.

For you, submitting means obeying regardless their reasons or mood. The exception is if they ask you to do something wrong. God did not give your folks complete authority over you because Jesus is still your Lord. But for everything else, if they ask you to do something, say "yes ma'am" or "yes, sir" and then do it.

Hopefully, your parents see how important it is for you to submit to their authority, and gently help you with that. But even if they don't, surprise them by doing what they ask. This is your training ground for a big future. This is your ticket to becoming your own boss and the boss of others.

There is no better time to learn to obey than now because a rebel-lion lurks in your heart and needs to be tamed. And the best way to tame it is to say "yes" to your folks. If you tame that lion now, you'll be able, when you are bigger, to tame the one who roams the earth, seeking dinner.

CHAPTER 6

As you obey your folks, a quiet confidence will grow in you because that's what living in a right relationship does. And as you do, your friends and others will sense something different about you and will treat you with respect. That respect, by the way, will further increase your sense of confidence.

> [2] *"Honor your father and mother"–this is the first commandment with a promise:* [3] *"so that it may be well with you and you may live long on the earth."*

And what starts as obeying "just because" will become in you an affirming, valuing attitude that I promise (no, God promises) will amaze you. Extra privileges and special treats now, and real freedom and authority later. God has designed all of life to work best when you focus on valuing Him and others more than yourself.

By obeying, you will discover that the one who honors God in this way, God will honor. His honor, by the way, is extravagant and apparent to everyone. You will sense that you are His favorite and, in fact, will be. For the present though, honoring your folks is God's path to prospering in everything you do and becoming successful for your entire life.

> [4] *And, fathers, do not provoke your children to anger, but bring them up in the discipline and instruction of the Lord.*

Now men, I am sorry that I need to come back to you again. I don't think that I'm piling on, but even if I am, you need it and can take it. While I told you to treat your wife as a person and not as a project, I must doubly emphasize this as it relates to your kids because they have project written all over them. Don't fall into that trap.

Your kids are not projects because projects are linear. Kids are not. The goal of a project is its completion. The goal for your children is the process and, in the process, a growing relationship.

Projects also have timetables that you establish. But with children, they establish the timing based on their development and ability to grasp concepts. Your job is to be aware of their capacity and be ready. While projects are controlled from the outside, that only works for a little while with your children. Get into their world and help them control themselves.

If you frustrate them with unrealistic demands, they will frustrate you. If you dump of them, they will dump on you. God, however, does not dump on you. He knows you and has developed a training regimen specifically designed for you. He's aware of what you can learn today so He doesn't try to teach tomorrow's lessons until you're ready.

So, take time to understand your children. Figure out how they learn and respond. Find out what motivates and dis-motivates them, and take time to teach them to obey. You will train your dog by creating time and space and games to teach obedience. Why not your children? Why do you wait until times of crisis when emotions are heightened? These moments are not optimal for learning.

If you establish your classroom on a regular basis, when they do disobey, your discipline will be an extension of their training and not a issue to deal with. What they learn in your classroom will be their reference point for real life, their entire life.

Your emotional reactions toward their behavior have far more consequences than all the Sunday school classes they attend. The cumulative effect of these face to face interactions, both good and bad, determines and reinforces what they come to believe about God, about life and themselves.

Don't you see that? Kindness will open their hearts. Anger, however, shuts their doors. Even though one of the purposes of adulthood is to overcome one's childhood, don't make it more difficult for them. Act like the adult in the room and bring them up to your level. Don't get on theirs.

> [5] *Slaves, obey your earthly masters with fear and trembling, in singleness of heart,*

Now there is one more set of relationships that I must address before I talk about the thrust of my letter, which is spiritual warfare. Your flesh and blood relationships are the final proving ground before you are ready to engage the devil and dislodge him from his strongholds. How can you submit to the Captain of the Lord's Army if you won't submit to the sergeants He has placed in your life?

CHAPTER 6

Employee/employer relationships might not look as covenantal or as important as familial ones because work is often not a choice, but a forced necessity. You do need to eat! But this relationship is as sacred, and as life changing, as your marriage if you are willing to see it that way.

I would go so far by saying that even if, God forbid, you were in so much debt that you had to sell yourself to another, this relationship would still be God-ordered and sacred, brimming with much potential to transform and infuse you with His power.

You see, relationships are God-designed crucibles. Those of you who had high school chemistry will remember that a crucible is a test tube into which dis-similar substances are put and to which fire is applied. The purpose of the crucible is to keep the materials together long enough for the fire to do its job and create something new.

But first, the fire will reveal the dross. In relationships, your selfish heart is exposed in a way nothing else can. If you don't view relationships as God-chosen vessels, you will do what you can to get out of the fire and sadly remain unchanged. That, by the way, is not God's intent for your life—you, unchanged. So, with His help, give yourself completely to your present employer even if you are looking for another job.

> *as you obey Christ;* [6] *not only while being watched, and in order to please them, but as slaves of Christ, doing the will of God from the heart.* [7] *Render service with enthusiasm, as to the Lord and not to men and women,*

For me, tent-making was that crucible. While I was being fast-tracked to be on top of the religious world, I had to go to the bottom to become a tentmaker. Because I had no visible means of support, I took a job as an apprentice with a boss I didn't much like and who didn't like me.

In fact, I thought that he felt that he owned me. He did not treat me as a person and pushed me hard. Nor was he kind—not one bit. But I chose to submit to him as if he was the kindest and most generous boss ever, like my Lord. The Spirit was teaching me that my natural life was not natural. It was my house of worship, and so I worshipped.

I wish I could say that this relationship ultimately changed him. It didn't; but it sure changed me. I discovered, in the confines of that sweat shop, a life that was refreshing and free. And when I finally left to establish my own business, I knew, because of him, how *not* to be a boss.

My employees love me, as do my clients, thanks to him. And I found that his critical eye has helped me focus on every stitch of each seam more than the finished product. Focusing on the details has earned me, and my tents, quite a reputation.

> [8] *knowing that whatever good we do, we will receive the same again from the Lord, whether we are slaves or free.*

I was getting a name for myself and started making some money. But more than that, the lessons the Holy Spirit taught me, while I was making tents, were more instructural and foundational than anything I learned in seminary. In fact, I'd say that my tent-making days is the reason I have been successful in my ministry because I still am tent-making.

When Barnabas knocked on my door, I was ready because instead of pieces of fabric, I began stitching saints together. You can see in this letter while the finished product is in view, I am looking at every stitch. And instead of mobile motels for businessmen, I am making, all over the world, places for God to put his head.

While I still make some money from time to time by making tents, what's awaiting me when my work for Him is finished is unimaginable. While I am not doing the Lord's work for gain, I know like a good boss, He has created bonus structures that will blow my mind and will blow yours as well, regardless the work He has assigned for you to do.

> [9] *And, masters, do the same to them. Stop threatening them, for you know that both of you have the same Master in heaven, and with him there is no partiality.*

This works the same for you bosses. Being over someone exposes the heart as much as being under someone. Having power

CHAPTER 6

over people who might not have the same passion and might resist you at times reveals your heart just like being told what to do.

I hope you realize that the Boss doesn't boss. I am amazed that the Sovereign, the Master of all things, would invite you, a speck of dust, to collaborate with Him in His work. The only way He controls, anyway, is by holding you in an open hand and getting inside of you. Other gods might exert control by squeezing, but not the Lord Jesus.

He must know something you don't as it relates to how to get your way. If you really want your employees to embrace your vision, it doesn't happen by force. Focus on growing them and they will grow your business. Treat them like a commodity and you will be ever looking over your shoulder, wondering what they are doing.

While it is obvious that you are in a better position than they are, don't overplay that hand because you really are in a symbiotic relationship. As they prosper, you prosper. And as you prosper, they should as well.

[10] *Finally,*

Now, let's get down to it. What I have written to this point leads to what I am about to say. I began this letter by telling you that I wanted you to live well in both the heavenly and the earthly realms. However, living well is not an end to itself. You were created to overturn some tables.

God placed you in Ephesus to displace the demons who reside there. But unless you know the Relational God and who you are "in Christ," unless you are able to live the exchanged life of "Christ in you" and unless you are living in the fullness of the Spirit, you will not be able to neuter the devil. That is why I have taken pains to pen this letter.

God has placed before you and within you a land flowing with milk and honey which you are to possess. But there are giants and strongholds, both within and without, who have been there for such a long time that they still think that they own the joint.

They might control a few things, but they don't own anything. By creation and redemption, Jesus has proven His ownership. And since the Lord has given to you both your own soul and Ephesus as your inheritance, they are yours if you are willing to take them. But these demonic entities are not going to easily give up what they have possessed for a long time.

be strong in the Lord and in the strength of his power.

That is why what I am about to say is not for the faint of heart. You will need to take your weaknesses and uncertainties and exchange them for His strength. And you will only be able to do this if you grow in your awareness of the absolute Lordship Jesus has over your life, your circumstances and over every demon who has ever dared challenge Him.

"Jesus is Lord" is a declaration not just for church; but for every day and in each situation that is contrary to His kingdom. "Jesus is Lord!" You can start by declaring this to yourself and to those areas in your life that are not quite right. Then take it to your family and work, and then to the streets and finally to the nations.

In doing so, you will invite the mightiness of His power to follow your words because His power resides in His Name and in your words. You also need to change your perception of yourself because the selfsame power that raised Jesus from the dead now resides in you.

[11] *Put on the whole armor of God, so that you may be able to stand against the wiles of the devil.*

When your heart and words resonate with the Lord's, demons are put on notice. Don't assume, however, when you awaken to the reality of warfare that they will scurry away. In fact, when demons become aware that someone is threatening their domain, they will pull out the specific playbook they have on that person.

They might arrange for those all too familiar temptations that trip you up to find you. They might whisper things about yourself or God that aren't true or create overwhelming circumstances which can flood you with a sense of helplessness or hopelessness. They will do anything to get you off-balance and give up, because that is their goal. Once you give up, they've won.

So, don't let them. You can protect yourself from their schemes. It might seem from your perspective that you are neither adequate

CHAPTER 6

nor have the right armor; but those lies are part of the devil's strategy to keep your eyes on your self. As long as you are looking at yourself or your circumstances, you're done. The devil's intent, as it has always been, is to separate close friends. And I can assure you that you can't be any closer to the Lord than you are now.

That's why I say, "Stand your ground." Your struggle is not about trying to win something or take something away from the devil. It is just the opposite. He is trying to get you to give up what God has already given. You need your eyes opened to this, and just hold on. This is what causes the devil to retreat.

Use everything God has provided to protect the most precious thing that He has given you–your sense of self. The demons will attack any chink you might have in your armor to get you questioning yourself and God. And let me tell you, your armor has a lot of chinks and that is why the Lord has given you His. It worked for Him. It works for me, and it will work for you. God has given you all the gear you need to fend off the demons who assault you, even

> [12] *For our struggle is not against enemies of blood and flesh, but against the rulers, against the authorities, against the cosmic powers of this present darkness, against the spiritual forces of evil in the heavenly places.*

the assaults that don't seem that demonic. Often times, their attacks are clothed in normal life. Sometimes demons will animate people to do their bidding in order to get you to react. At other times, they might arrange circumstances to upset you. Be aware of this. People or happenstances might be the vehicle, but it could just be that demons are driving the car. If you get caught up in reacting to people or circumstances rather than responding to God, the demons have you right where they want.

Jesus didn't fall into this trap. He knew that the darkness which blanketed the sun and swirled around the cross was the entirety of the demonic cabal descending on Him. Though He felt, like Job, that His Father had forsaken Him, Jesus knew that this wasn't true because His Father was in Him reconciling the world to Himself.

While the demons tried to shroud His soul and separate Him from the awareness of the Father's love, Jesus covered Himself with what He knew of His Father. "You have not despised the affliction of the afflicted and You certainly are not hiding Your face from Me!"[1] In the darkest moments of His soul, Jesus stood His ground and defeated the demonic cabal on the cross.

From the demons who nip at your heels to the princes who seek to drive a stake in your heart to the ones who sit in the stands to direct and cheer them on, the intent of this cabal is to destroy anyone who threatens their domain. They have many resources at their disposal and won't think twice about using them.

> [13] *Therefore, take up the full armor of God, so that you will be able to resist in that evil day,*

This awareness will make you see the need to forget your paltry efforts to hold your life together. They fight with lasers. Your sticks will not protect you or yours, so learn to use God's armor.

Regardless the intensity of the assault, don't doubt the effectiveness of God's armor because the devil would love for you to lay the Lord's down, pick yours up again and run for your life. Even if all hell breaks loose, this evil cabal is nothing against you because you are as protected as Jesus is. And once the waves go over you, they will roll back out to the sea while you remain standing.

> *and having done everything, to stand firm.*

And stand, you must. God has placed you right in the middle of your inheritance and has called you to defend what He has given. Look at your soul. Look around at your relationships. Look at your neighborhood. Look at your finances. Look at your ministry. Look at your future. God has already given them to you. You needn't plead with God. He is not the one trying to keep them from you or take them away.

Yes, there are things you must do, and I will delineate them for you now; but your victory is rooted in "it is finished" and not "try harder." God has already accomplished the work. You have already won. What is left for you to do is to doubt your doubts, believe the truth about yourself and resist the enemy by faith.

---

1. Psalm 22:24

CHAPTER 6

> [14] *Stand therefore, and fasten the belt of truth around your waist,*

You might think that you will need a lot of firepower to defeat the devil, but you would be wrong. Since "one little word will fell him,"[2] I will leave the only offensive weapon God has provided for last.

Anyway, I am sure you have heard the adage, "The best offense is a good defense." This is even truer in spiritual warfare because, again, you are not trying to gain anything. The devil's strategy is to trick you into giving up what God has already given.

The first thing you need to know about the devil's strategy is that it is based entirely on a lie and that he is banking on you to let your feelings instruct your faith, rather than the other way around. That is why the first piece of armor you are to put on is the belt of truth. Each piece of armor, whether defensive or offensive, is attached to this belt, so you can see how important this is. Truth ties everything together.

It doesn't matter whether demons try to trip you up by getting you to think that you're neither good enough nor able, it all comes back to lies. That is why I have taken pains to write this letter to you. I wanted to dispel the shadows that keep you in the dark, and ineffective.

To recount, (and I have no problem going over this again) I have been telling you the truth about the Relational God, His grace and your inclusion. And the truth about the cross. And the truth about Jesus. And the truth about overcoming your propensities. Also the truth about being filled with the Spirit. The truth about the new humanity and the truth about you.

I know that you need to hear and rehear these truths again and again. You might need to go back and reread what I wrote so it can sink in because this is what the devil does not want you to know. He knows that these truths will supercharge you.

But you will need to put the belt on. It can't be left hanging in your locker. You need to be as intentional putting this on, as a soldier who puts on his warrior mindset before going into battle.

---

2. Martin Luther, "A Mighty Fortress is our God."

For you, it can be as simple as singing, "Jesus loves me, this I know." It can be as simple as telling your soul to hope in the Lord. It can be as simple as lifting your voice in praise to God. It's as simple (and as hard) as persuading and encouraging your heart before Him. David did just that when his men picked up rocks to stone him. You can too, and you must.

and put on the breastplate of righteousness.

The armor God provides will protect you from potential harm caused by specific attacks. If an enemy has landmines, an undercarriage that is impervious to explosions is needed. If they have heat seeking missiles, you must have decoy flares to throw them off their track. The devil has weapons which have worked on mankind from the beginning. As you become aware of them, your appreciation for type of defenses the Lord has given you will grow.

The devil's primary attack is to lie about who you are. It worked on Adam and Eve when the devil suggested they were less than what God created. They were however, as you are, made in God's image, vitally connected to Him and all that He has, and with a destiny angels desire. The devil's MO is to besmirch God and keep you off balance by telling you what you and God are not.

That is why you must first protect your heart, your inner person, from any thought that tells you that you are less. You need to protect your vital organs because without a breastplate, a soldier can easily have the wind knocked out of him or worse. Your breastplate is the righteousness of God.

Understanding who you are is as essential as knowing who God is, and to know God's righteousness is to know your own. If you don't know the truth about yourself and your blood-washed perfections, you will never be able to rebut the devil's accusations or be a threat to him. In fact, acknowledging God's rightness without embracing your own is like trying to walk on one foot.

From time to time, I do remind myself of my past and the pit from which I was dug. And once in a great while, I will weep at the bent of my heart. That is right and proper because I need to remember His great mercy. But it is not right for me to agree with the condemner, condemning. It is not right to listen to lies.

CHAPTER 6

Though I sin, I am not a sinner. Though I might struggle with my old nature from time to time, that is not who I am. That nature was co-crucified with the last Adam and I now have the nature of the second Man who sits enthroned. I am righteous and a saint, the one greatly loved by the One who left heaven's pleasures to find a bride. And he found His bride in me!

So how can I sully the image of God in which I am made by agreeing with the devil and think less of me than God does? It is not pride to think this way. It is pride not to.

Since your default position is to doubt your own rightness, you need to convince yourself by reading yourself into the word. No one else can do that for you. As I have said before, you are the best preacher you will ever hear. So, take the words of Jeremiah and prophesy to yourself, "Hear what the Lord says, 'Before the womb, I knew you and have appointed you.'"

Tell yourself that God is making your feet like the feet of a mountain goat and is causing you to walk upon your high places. Tell yourself that you are His beloved and that He is yours. Why not? Has what you have been doing worked for you? Well, this has worked for me.

And be the best audience you can ever have. Receive and believe the word spoken to you by you. This is putting on the breastplate of righteousness, and you will find when the devil sends a projectile your way, it won't be received because you will know that it is not the truth. Too many times, things which should harmlessly bounce off, become a crisis you need to deal with because you do not know how to protect your heart.

> [15] *As shoes for your feet put on whatever will make you ready to proclaim the gospel of peace.*

The next thing you will need to do is protect is your feet. Without sure footing you will continually be off balance and not able to stand, let alone advance. A large reason many fall and few advance is fear, especially the fear of failure.

While the breastplate shields your sense of self, boots safeguard what you are about. As I mentioned earlier, you were created both with great value and unimaginable significance because God created you both to be and do. These first two pieces of armor address both because these are the main struggles of your life. Demons know this and will capitalize on your weak spots any way they can.

While you can assure your heart about who you are, you cannot assure yourself into your destiny. You must take steps outside of your comfort zone to do that. That is why the Christian life is a life of risk. (If you are not risking, by the way, don't be surprised when God finds a way to help you out of the nest.)

God has called you to risk your life for Him because it comes with a promise of His presence and that He will not fail you. But the uncertainty can seem so real and the exposure more than most are willing to chance. And the devil will, in moments of decision, magnify the obstacles and minimize both your own stature and God's to keep you neutralized by fear.

That is why you need the peace that comes from protecting your feet because you can be sure that when you begin to move in a direction, stuff will happen. Life always tests your commitments and the devil always resists. You will also stub your toe from time to time.

So, don't dig up in the dark what you have sown in the light. You must not doubt the decisions you make before the Lord. A double minded man is at war with himself and does the devil's work for him. Anxiety and fear, self-doubt and paralysis should be external to you. Sometimes, however, these feelings are the atmosphere in which you live.

The good news is the One who washes your feet has also given you His shoes. Jesus has put all things that concern your destiny under His feet and yours. Before time began, He planned your path. He has gone before and is waiting to meet you at your destination; and He is carrying you. He has taken all the pressure off.

So, venture out and begin taking steps toward your call. You may have to speak peace to the troubled sea from time to time; but keep going and you will discover a deep-seated peace that will keep you going, regardless the waves.

This good news is first for you. You can walk in rest in the midst of a storm. And once you experience this, this message will be the good news you share with others.

CHAPTER 6

> ¹⁶ *With all of these, take the shield of faith, with which you will be able to quench all the flaming arrows of the evil one.* (the word shield in Greek is door)

These pieces of armor will keep you safe most of the time. But once in a while, a demon will zing you with something that you don't expect, and you will find yourself tempted to take offence at someone or something. There's not much that burns as hotly as an offence. And once an offence is taken, it keeps smoldering.

That is why you need to have ready at all times, the mother of all protective gear—the shield of faith. And I am not talking about a namby-pamby shield that fits on your arm which you must continually move this way and that in order to keep from getting hit. Talk about the need for being hyper-vigilant and looking for demons under every rock! You are to be aware and alert, but not in this way.

No, the shield that God has given you is as big as a door. You are to plant it right in front of you. That's right, between you and the cabal, a big honking shield that is impervious to projectiles. Your job is not to try to fend off each attack, but to stay behind it.

If you rely on your own faith to ward off these arrows, you will find that you are not agile enough, nor your faith sufficient enough to withstand the onslaughts hidden in the unexpected, undesired and unrelenting situations that arise. The secret of overcoming is having a faith as big as Jesus. He told his disciples to have the faith of God and I am telling you that His faith is your shield.

That's why I have talked about living an exchanged life. I didn't realize this possibility right away, but when I saw that my life is hidden with Christ in God and that I live by the life of Another, my whole world changed.

I now daily exchange my weakness for His strength, the meagerness of my life for the fullness of His and His faith for mine. This "it's me, but really not me" paradigm will seem confusing to you until you experience what I have. But when the Holy Spirit reveals it to you, you will know.

I learned how to stay behind this shield, by the way, from David, the worshipping warrior. He placed the Lord, his shield, before Him at all times whether he was tending sheep or bringing down a giant. Now there were times when he didn't, and you can see how he opened himself up to hurtful attacks. While you can learn from these sloppy times, I'd rather focus on the times David did make the Lord his shield.

David prioritized and cultivated the presence of the Lord wherever he was, and in whatever situation he found himself. His desire for the Presence overpowered propriety. Whether taking food which belonged only to priests, dancing foolishly before the masses with hardly anything on or taking the ark of God's presence from behind the veil home with him, David did not accept the Old Covenant proscriptions.

While others thought God mouthed "no," David heard one big, "yes!" What barriers? The veils which kept everyone else away were entry points for David. Nothing was going to keep David from the intimacy he desired, even if he needed to live in the New Testament while everyone else lived in the Old. Regardless the rules and regulations, David saw the heart of God because he walked by faith and not by sight. And he worshipped. Oh, how he worshipped!

And that is the key for you as well. Nothing protects you from the devil's zingers as worshipping the One before you. Learn, like David did, to express your heart while no one is looking. Take David's words and make them your own. If you make up little ditties and sing them back to the Lord, you will soon be conducting a symphony! And as you do, you will realize more and more that while you are engaging your faith this way, the Lord's faith is operating and moving in and through you, as only He can.

[17] *Take the helmet of salvation,*

Now I need to talk about one more piece of armor before I discuss the sword. And that piece is your helmet. Your helmet is provided to keep you thinking straight. Faith has a logic to it, you know. Without faith, life can become confusing because it often seems like one big non sequitur after another.

You need a Rosetta Stone to interpret life because life speaks in a foreign language. God's salvation is the primer which allows you to make sense of life and cooperate with Him. Too often salvation is presented as just an event which happened when you gave your life

CHAPTER 6

to Him. But it is so much more. It is also a destination and a process. When you adopt this salvation mindset, you will be able to interpret circumstances in a way that will keep you going even when there is every reason not to.

First, a salvation mindset brings you into a growing knowledge and awareness of the Person who calls you, and on whom you call. Then, it centers your thoughts around the beauty that you are becoming rather than focusing on the ashes you once were. And finally, understanding the process of salvation keeps your heart settled as everything around you shifts. That is why the helmet of salvation consists of a who, a what and a how.

The who, of course, is Jesus. From the first act of creation to His final return, Jesus has and always will intervene in the affairs of men. And the gospel is that He still personally intervenes, just as decisively, in your life as well. He is the One on whom you can call whenever you feel threatened. He is the One who rips open the heavens and comes to your rescue when you cry out.

And the more He captures your imagination, the clearer your vision will become. You will not only see Him more clearly, but your perception of yourself will also grow and the size of your obstacles will shrink.

The who of salvation is also the what because Jesus is not only your Savior, He also is your salvation. Jesus is who you are going to look like when God is done restoring all things. He is the blueprint to which the Spirit refers when orchestrating the events of your life. Jesus is what your future you, the fully saved you, looks like.

As the Old Testament types foreshadow Christ, so Christ foreshadows you. Jesus is a type of you because when He appears, you will be like Him for you will see Him as He is. To the extent that Jesus is revealed to you here, the more you will reflect him here. This is the reason theology is the most practical subject you can ever study because when you study God, you glimpse yourself.

But while knowing the who and what is important, they are not enough. You also need to know how salvation is worked out so you can fully cooperate with God's work in your life. If you don't know the process, you will resist the very circumstances which come to change you. Understanding salvation from God's perspective creates a storyline into which you can see yourself written, and only then you can rest in the process.

This is why I preach Christ and Him crucified. In fact, when I was in Corinth, Jesus and the cross was all I talked about for 18 months. I don't want to brag but I never ran out of material; and I could have talked more if I wasn't run out of town. Jesus is the who and the what, and the cross is the how.

The cross is the upside-down logic of God because it is the way God enacts all that He seeks to accomplish. Through death comes life. Becoming smaller makes you bigger. Losing your reputation gives you influence. Giving away all, enriches. Weakness is strength and foolishness is wisdom. Losing control gives authority. Up is down and down is up.

The cross of Christ embodies these principles and is how God works, in you, what has been accomplished in Jesus. He brings you to the end of yourself so you can find the beginnings of God. As this principle becomes clearer to you, you will glory in the cross as much as I do.

The cross became my close companion when I discovered the grace of God in the desert of Arabia. There God broke me and changed me. There I learned how not to depend on myself. There I learned the principle of the cross.

Since then I have accelerated the process by desiring weakness and by rejoicing in the weakness the cross brings. I die daily and yet I live. This is the gospel I proclaim! This is the salvation I teach! Christ and Him Crucified. The who, the what, and the how.

and the sword of the Spirit, which is the word of God.

Now with the helmet and the rest of the armor in place, you are ready to attack the strongholds which keep people imprisoned. The demons Jesus defanged on the cross still hold onto their little fiefdoms and the precious people entrapped within their municipalities. I told you that demons are not going to easily give up what they have inhabited and ruled from the beginning of time.

Why do you think God created mankind in the first place? Do you think the nascent earth was a blissful retreat, or at minimum neutral, when Adam and Eve arrived on the scene? Hardly. If

CHAPTER 6

it were, God would not have told them to subdue as it relates to the world or protect as it relates to the garden.

These sound like fighting words because they are. The word "rule" is not genteel. It describes a battle where one is left standing and the other enslaved. It means to forcibly subjugate. It is even used to describe rape which is the ultimate expression of a complete and humiliating domination of a weaker by a stronger. Does this make the world sound like a safe place?

And why would Adam and Eve be commanded to protect a garden if it wasn't under threat? No, paradise was not what it seemed. Eden was not a place to frolic, but a place to learn principles of warfare before traveling on its rivers to displace the demons who had established municipalities all over the planet.

And here you are, millennia later, in Ephesus. Some things haven't changed. The culture created by these self-same demons still permeates your city and keeps your neighbors in line. And the system devised by the devil to meet their temporary needs with the toys he's scattered to keep the chattel distracted, remain.

And since those in this world system still sit on the devil's lap, to a great extent, his work is already done for him. The cabal has created enough rabbits to chase and enough idols to worship to keep everyone chasing their own tails and harried.

What has changed is this–the doors are no longer locked because the keys are no longer his. The Stronger has already humiliated the weaker. Yes, the doors are guarded, but they're open. You are to disperse those who block entry so the souls Jesus came to save can see the light of day. Remember, the cabal can do nothing to hurt you so use your sword put the hurt on them and get them to move out of the way.

But just as you cannot protect yourself with your own armor, neither can you disperse the cabal with your own sword. God has given you His own, the Spirit's sword, which has been tested in the fiercest of contests. The Spirit's sword is the word of God, mind you, not the thoughts of God.

Thoughts are important, but as it relates to warfare, thoughts will not move the needle. What is on the inside must find its way out for demons to yield. When the Lord returns, the sword will proceed from His mouth because it is sheathed there. Learn to unsheathe yours.

Nor can you just say anything and expect the demons to move. Quoting any old verse will not cause a stir, just like a lock will not open for any key. The key must be lock specific. The word you speak must be specific as well, if your words are to loosen the demon's grip.

This means you must be attentive to the Spirit's voice because the sword you grasp is the Rhema of God, the God-whispered word, and not the Logos, the general written word, however precious it is. The written word Jesus heard and fed on in the wilderness became the sword He used when confronted by the devil.

So be attentive to the voice of the Spirit when you open the Word. Ask Him to help you hear because He speaks. When a thought impresses you, take note of it and begin to dialogue with Him about it. And protect these words because these are the verses the Spirit will bring to your mind at the right time.

Spirit-born words are the grace bombs which open hearts to the possibility of God. Wherever Jesus went, faith was sparked in people because God's immediate presence in Christ was accompanied by a specific word. And God hasn't changed His ways, only those through whom He works. When the Spirit and His Word become an extension of you, you will have the same effect on people and devils that Jesus had.

[18] *Pray in the Spirit at all times in every prayer and supplication.*

But pray, pray, pray!! Praying is required because warfare has you navigating unfamiliar domains, full of smokescreens and landmines. That is why you need help from the One who sees.

But make sure you are not just praying from your mind. Praying needs a rational basis, for sure, but it also needs an emotional tie. Your head needs to be attatched to your heart because praying one without the other will not be as effective. Too often Christians land on one side or the other-either praying perfectly scripted, reserved prayers or ones with just a lot of bluster.

CHAPTER 6

Remember, praying is not only to move God's heart, but to open yours as well. So, find your voice in His words. God is attracted to His Word and comes to anyone, anywhere, anytime and in any situation where His Word is uttered. Develop your prayer life by rooting it in the prayers scattered throughout the Scriptures. (One of the best ways, by the way, to become a theologian is to pray the Scriptures.)

But don't stop there. Take the great prayers of Scripture and add a great big "Oh!" to them for yourself. See yourself as the starving beggar needing bread. See yourself as the widow ignored by justice. Neither the kingdom of darkness nor the kingdom of heaven is taken without some violence, so stamp your foot and say "I am not going anywhere, until . . ."

Take the word and supplicate for discernment. For direction. For fearlessness and encouragement. For breakthroughs. For signs and wonders. For the souls of men and women. You only need to ask for your daily bread, but for everything else, pray like it is dependent upon you because in some measure, it is.

And also, pray from your spirit. Praying in the spirit goes deeper than both your mind and emotions because your spirit is that part of you which is vitally connected with the eternal Spirit of God who knows and reveals, convinces and dispels the darkness.

Your part is to sense the Spirit's leadings in order to collaborate with Him in His work. Praying from your spirit helps you do that. For myself, I pray to the extent of my understanding and then, with my spirit, I pray to the extent of God's.

Your spirit is that place where you and the Triune intermingle. This is most remarkable—you and the Triune sharing space, sharing life. How big that space must be!!! How sacred! How important! How immediate the Presence! It is from this place that I am asking you to pray.

Praying in spirit is similar in some ways to regular praying because whether it's your body, your soul or spirit, you give expression of that part of you in prayer. You pray with your body when you kneel or lift your hands. You disclose your soul when you put into words your thoughts and feelings. In the same way, praying in spirit gives voice to your spirit.

But your spirit communicates differently from your other parts. Your body and soul are, at times, loud and insistent and difficult to ignore. But not your spirit. When your body tells you how it is doing or what it wants, you know because you understand body-words. You also have a fairly good idea whether your soul is up or down, anxious or excited because you know its language. Your spirit, however, speaks softly and in a way that you must learn to recognize.

And of all people, you should know what praying in spirit is because when I first visited Ephesus, God made it abundantly clear to you. Our first discussion was centered on your confusion about baptisms. You were aware of John's baptism and the need to be serious about God. And boy, were you!

But when I told you about Jesus and you received Him, the Spirit immediately immersed you into Christ, after which I baptized you in water. But then after that, I placed my hands on you and the Spirit came on you and you began to speak words that you did not understand–spirit-words. While you didn't understand what you were saying, God did.

While I want all of you to speak spirit-words, you can pray from your spirit without these words because praying in spirit is both a principle and a practice. I would be hard pressed to say which is more important because the principle is so important. I know of some assemblies that just babble and call it spiritual. They misinterpret the public and private use of spirit-words.

The principle of praying in spirit is complete dependence upon God. I hope you have seen this thread run throughout my entire letter. It finds its highest expression in prayer because prayer is where you present yourself to God. You don't need to say much in His presence, just from your heart, "Lord, here I am. I desire and need you." That is enough to begin.

Cultivate brokenness and transparency. Tell God you need Him in everything, even in your praying. Make yourself small so He can enlarge you. From your deepest part, groan your lack and desire God, only God. And as you exercise your spirit in this way, both an awareness of God will grow, as will little revelations that

CHAPTER 6

you are to plant in your own soul to grow. You will also begin to sense little impressions which you are to obey.

But praying in spirit is more than a principle. It is also a practice which you can do by praying spirit-words. When you couple the principle with the practice, you open yourself up a whole new line of communication, one that is unfiltered because it bypasses your limited understanding and your fickle feelings.

As I have said, when you pray in spirit-words, your spirit gives expression to the things that are in your spirit. Sometimes it's worship. Sometimes it's praying about God's business. At other times, you declare mysteries that the Spirit will disclose to your conscious later. And sometimes when I pray from my spirit, there is such a vehemence that I know I am engaging the enemy. And I also know that God has given this to me so I can keep my battery charged.

Let me tell you, I credit praying spirit-words as much as anything for the revelations God has given me, and with my effectiveness and the ability to press on when the whole world is pressing against me. If the spirit is flowing out of me, how can the world not move out of the way?

That is why I prioritize praying this way. But you wouldn't know that I am a spirit-word fanatic because when I am around you, I speak Greek because you are my audience. But when I am by myself, my audience is God.

For those who have not yet spoken spirit-words, listen to me. Don't beat yourself up or have someone guilt you into trying. That is not the Spirit. But don't settle either. If this is (and it is) of God, why not say, "Why not me?"

And you needn't have me there to put my hands on you. The Spirit has already been poured out upon you. You already have permission. As with your salvation, come to Jesus who not only forgives but immerses in the Spirit, and open your heart to Him afresh, hungering for this gift.

Then just like salvation, receive it by faith. Faith to receive the Spirit in this way has the same two components as receiving anything from the Lord. The first is to engage the Giver by saying, "Yes, this gift is also mine. Thank you that you have already given the Spirit to me and that I have already received the ability to speak from my spirit."

The second is acting on your faith. Everything God gives is received this way, so don't think that this most precious gift is any different. Give your tongue to God and begin speaking in heaven's language. You can't speak in Greek and in tongues as the same time so begin speaking in the new language God has given you.

It will seem foolish at first, but what God-thing isn't? For some of you, a Spirit-flow will immediately follow. For others, it might sound like, "Gaga, goo-goo." But regardless, continue praying spirit-words by faith and you will discover what I have—an added depth and effectiveness in your prayer life, and in all of life.

> *To that end keep alert and always persevere in supplication for all the saints.*

And as you attend to yourself in prayer, don't forget about your brothers and sisters. Pray that they learn what you have about keeping yourself in the love of God because that is the essence of warfare. Pray that the love of God overwhelms their consciousness.

Pray for all of them, the ones you get along with and the ones you don't. Pray for those you know and those you don't. Pray because God wants more than a people to govern and call His own. He desires a people to indwell. Unless each one you know how to keep yourself in God's love, this will remain a theory, at best.

My entire life has been given to this end: to see the body of Christ complete and standing together because the body of Christ is the endpoint of Scriptures. Regardless where you put your finger in the Scripture, you find God's burning desire is not only to be with man, but to indwell and animate them.

That is why I am up nights on end with my eyes wide open. I am so aware of God's heart that I must do what I can to ensure that He has a welcoming place to dwell. I am asking that you also pray with me,

> [19] *Pray also for me, so that when I speak, a message may be given to me to make known with boldness the mystery of the gospel,*

CHAPTER 6

and for me. I am not as put together as you might think. I find myself, at times, in situations where I have a desire to tell people about Jesus, but I neither see an opening nor does anything come to mind. But I find that if I open my mouth, God gives me words.

Keep praying that this continues for I don't take anything for granted. I am in desperate need of His help and your prayers. Even in jail where I know everyone, God still must show me which part of the gospel to proclaim because what reaches one does not impact all.

Yes, I proclaim Jesus' death and resurrection, but my message is not one-note because the cross isn't nor are people. Each one who enters my cell is different with a different history. I have found that the gospel is not a rigid box into which all must squeeze. It is a knit fabric which takes the shape of the person listening. Therefore, I try to take God's amazing message and personally match it the ones in front of me regardless their mindset.

My friend Onesimus, for example, would never have opened his heart to Jesus if I told him that he was a rebellious sinner. That part of the gospel was for another time and another place, and when he was ready. A sinner, whom God was mad at, was not the door opener for him. Anyway, I think he already knew that he blew it and was mad at himself and the world, and probably God.

No. When he saw how free I was and didn't understand how I could be this way chained between two guards, Onesimus and I began dialoguing. I realized that part of the reason he was a slave was because he had no self-worth. While Onesimus hated being a slave, he couldn't run from it because in his own mind, he was.

I told him Jesus' death on the cross was the measure of his worth and proved God's love for him. This was new information for Onesimus and it messed with his slavish mind.

But now, Onesimus gets it. He has a slave mentality no more. You will want to talk with him and hear how the gospel has affected his life before he leaves your fellowship for Colossae to deliver my letter to his master.

All I know is that Onesimus wants to resume his position as a slave and asked to be the one handing the letter to Philemon. It is always a mystery to me what part of the gospel God uses to enter the lives of people and how that good news expands within a heart to become a living message. That's why I have asked you to pray for me because I want to be used more and more this way by the Spirit.

> [20] *for which I am an ambassador in chains. Pray that I may declare it boldly, as I must speak.*

Onesimus now realizes that, as a slave, he has a greater platform to speak to everyone because everyone is enslaved by the world's belief system. His freedom within will cause others to take notice. His embrace of sonship while still being a slave will shake the foundations of Colossae's power structure. The powers that be won't know what to do with his life or message. And this will lead others to salvation.

And just like Onesimus, my imprisonment punctuates the good news that I declare as well. But, as you know, life in jail can be a grind and when it is, I tend to grow silent. Part of the reason I wrote this letter anyway was to encourage myself in the things I know and believe.

And I also have another ulterior motive. As you get stronger and the Spirit makes these words come alive in you, I will have better prayer partners. It's ok to have secret motives and some self-interest because God does as well.

As I have re-read parts of this letter, I am convicted to speak even more boldly because it is black and white to me. Light versus Darkness. It's a clash of two kingdoms diametrically opposed to each other. And more and more, I see my role as a spokesman for God's government, so I need to be clear and confident each and every time I speak. For this, please pray.

> [21] *So that you also may know how I am and what I am doing, Tychicus will tell you everything. He is a dear brother and a faithful minister in the Lord.*

So that's it. I have gotten it off my chest. There are a few personal things I want to tell you, but not in this letter because I want you to make some copies of this and send it off to the other churches. Some of the things I want to share with you are not for public consumption, but for you, my friends.

CHAPTER 6

Tychicus will fill you in on everything that is happening with me and will answer all your questions. I trust you will go out of your way to make him feel at home. He has been such a good friend and encouragement to me. Tychicus could have been spending his time in Rome by making his own way; but he chose to hang with me and my two guards. This, by the way, has also started the guards wondering what gets into people who encounter Jesus.

> [22] *I am sending him to you for this very purpose, to let you know how we are, and to encourage your hearts.*

So, please avail yourself of him while he is there. You will be refreshed by his presence just as I have been because he is a breath of fresh air! And I think his coming to you is timely. I have sensed some stagnation there, as I have said. It could be that your questions about the incongruity of my condition have opened the door to this discouragement. Tychicus will put that to rest and get the wind blowing again. God is still on the throne and He still is good!

> [23] *Peace be to the whole community, and love with faith, from God the Father and the Lord Jesus Christ.* [24] *Grace be with all who have an undying love for our Lord Jesus Christ.*

As I close this letter, let me invoke a blessing on you. This blessing is the summation of everything I have written. And as I pronounce this blessing over you, God is putting His hand on you, so open your hearts and receive this from Him.

"May the One who has ever lived in community, saturate you with His presence and may you live with Him in heavens' atmosphere right there in Ephesus. And may the love which the Father and Son enjoy play out in your midst. May His favor flavor you in such a way that you would be known for a love which produces life wherever you go. And may grace pile up upon grace."

As I have opened this letter, so I close it. Blessed be God and blessed are you.

AFTERWORD

You might ask me whether I believe this stuff or not. First, let me say that we are all trying to figure this out, I hope. Personally, I don't want to rest on the laurels of Athanasius of Alexandria or Calvin or N.T. Wright however great they might be. While I do want to learn from them, God has given me Himself to explore.

Tozer said, "We tend by a secret law of the soul to move toward our mental image of God. This is true not only of the individual Christian, but of the company of Christians that composes the Church. Always the most revealing thing about the Church is her idea of God."[1]

So, it is imperative that each of us grapple with who God is and by extension, who we are. You and I were created to be theologians. This book has been part of my continuing effort. And I know that if the Lord would grant me more years and I would revisit Ephesians a decade from now, it would look different because I would be different. His Word does not change, but as it changes me, the Word changes in me. The Word becomes more fleshy or real. God becomes more incarnate in me. But, as to whether I believe this stuff or not, I would ask, "Which stuff?"

That the Trinitarian relationship is most wonderfully delightful and the primary motivation for everything God is about, and, as such, should be a significant focus of the church? Yes. Reading between the lines of Scripture, the Triune's relationship must be

---

1. A.W. Tozer, "The Knowledge of the Holy" (New York: HarperCollins, 1978)

AFTERWORD

David and Johnathan's on steroids, Naomi and Ruth's multiplied exponentially and so much more than Adam and Eve's in the garden.

These are types of God as much as Joseph and David are types of Christ. So, the image of God refers as much to their relationship as it does to their individuality. When Genesis 5:1–2 talks about being made in His image, scriptures refers to both the singular and to the collective, individuals living in community (male and female, created He them.) The relationship the Father and Jesus enjoys is as much the image of God, and maybe more, than looking at the specific attributes of God.

But the church is fuzzy on the Trinitarian relationship and mankind's part in it. Because of this, the church's theology tends to center around either a redemptive theme or a kingdom theme. If your theology begins with the fall, your purpose and the purpose of the church will largely be colored by redemption with your message both "sinner saved by grace" and sanctification.

If it begins with the creation and mankind's part in ruling, then taking back the kingdom with the need for its accompanying power will be emphasized. In 1 John, John acknowledges these when he talks about little children knowing that their sins are forgiven (redemption) and young men, being strong and overcoming the devil (kingdom-restoring).

While these are important, John points beyond the fall and beyond creation, back into eternity and into the heart of the Father. "Fathers, you have known Him who is from the beginning." It is this mystery which the church is called to explore. And in that exploration, hearts are made right and the kingdom comes.

In the beginning, there was fellowship–the fellowship of the Father and Son in the Spirit—the same fellowship that you and I were called into. Paul, in 1 Corinthians 1:9, says that (literally) you were called into *the* fellowship of *the* Son. With whom has the Son been sharing life forever and what is the nature of that relationship?

The church has largely left this aspect of God unexplored, and because of that, has a skewed view of man. While man needs to be redeemed and while you are here to displace the devil, the reason for man is God, and the church must wrestle with this as well.

AFTERWORD

That God perceives me as an equal with a small "e"? Yes, if the reason for man is God, then likes can only have a satisfying relationship with likes. You and Fido only go so far, but if you were created for the bridal chamber, what sort of creation are you?

With our rightful aversion to pride, we might be throwing the baby out with the bath water when we minimize son-ship and embrace sinner-ship. What God says about you is so amazingly wonderful and unbelievable, could it be that He is the one who is heretical?

That His grace is so over the top that it too is heretical? His grace must be as other as He is, beyond my ability to grasp and so wonderfully wonderful that it will cause me to worship Him forever. At least, I sure hope it is and I want to have more grace bombs dropped on me so I can experience it here.

That the Father did *not* turn His face from Jesus on the cross? Yes, I do. I am convinced that the darkened sun was the entirety of the evil cabal descending on Christ to destroy Him as Paul states in Colossians and not His Father rejecting Him. Regardless, like any good dad, the Father would never deal harshly with His Son in public.

The death of Christ is more nuanced than you have come to believe. But if you would understand the three-fold nature of the offerings on the Day of Atonement and the triune nature of man, you would have gathered some clues as to what happened, and where and why.

Anyway, Paul says that God was in Christ reconciling the world unto Himself, not being angry with mankind or His Son. It was God in the hands of angry sinners, not the other way around. His restorative wrath *was* poured out upon Christ's soul so that God could obliterate the old sin nature. But this was done in private when His soul went to hell, not on the cross. The two goats on the day of atonement speak of this as does Psalm 22 and Psalm 88.

The cross was the place where mankind did our worst toward God. And there, God removed all of our excuses because on the cross He showed nothing but love. The cross was also the place where He defeated the demonic cabal. If you are curious about this, download the article, "The Deaths of Jesus" on the book's website, www.ephesiansjazz.com.

That the entire purpose for creation and redemption was to create community? 100 percent. Creating oneness in diversity is how

AFTERWORD

God glorifies Himself, and community is what happens when God shows up. All other pursuits in His Name whose end is not focused on forming community might be short-sighted. A good movie to watch that brings this point to the forefront is "Woodlawn." I typically don't like Christian movies, but this is one of the great exceptions.

That your natural gifts and abilities hinder the kingdom more than they help, if left unbroken? Again 100 percent. Whether a leader or servant type, it doesn't matter. God must touch your natural strength like He did Jacob's, or you will remain unchanged and your ministry will remain natural, not spiritual. Watchman Nee understood this better than anyone whom I have read, so if you are curious, invest in a few of his books. "Changed into His Likeness" is a good place to start. And if you are a minister of God's word and haven't read "The Ministry of the Word," you really need to.

That doctrine is *not* God's primary concern? This is a little dicey, but there are reasons God has put seemingly conflicting statements in Scripture. One big reason is to reveal how little we know and encourage some humility. Anyway, God is the only one who can talk through both sides of His mouth and still be right.

But don't hear what I am not saying. Doctrine is important. But could it be that doctrine is firstly and primarily for the heart and not the head? If that is the case, for example, my heart can rest when I hear that God will never leave me nor forsake me, eternally saved as it were. I can also be motivated at the same time to be careful when I hear that I can be cut off. David didn't involve himself in things that were too big for him. Trying to defend a position when you really don't have the entirety of God's mind might be a bit big for you, don't you think?

That the devil pre-existed man on earth and ruled it? Yeah. I think so. I am an unashamed *gapper*, so part of my framework is that Genesis 1:2 is the effect of a cause. The effect was darkness, chaos and confusion. The cause was the demonic cabal. The devil who once was the lead worshipper in a previous age rebelled and took control of the earth while God vacated His dwelling. It then became as empty and chaotic as he is. (I love big stories like this anyway.)

So, for me, Genesis 1:2 is an "and it came to pass" moment when God, after a long, long time began to intervene to take back

AFTERWORD

His earth from the usurper and He created the woman and man to be His instruments. This is the only thing that makes sense to me as it relates to the age of the earth and to the chaos and emptiness the earth was found in. A universe that has existed for billions of years and a re-creation of seven literal days is not outside the realm of possibility. But I could be wrong.

That the marriage relationship and relationships in general are God's test tube to create heaven on earth? Yes. My favorite quote in all the world is from the great 20th century philosopher, Homer Simpson. He said, "To alcohol–the cause of and solution to all of life's problems." If you change the word "alcohol" to "relationships," this quote becomes absolutely true. My wife and I have discovered the cause and solution to all of life's problems and have found that the power of God, rooted in His Word, is great enough to overcome all the things that can keep a deep-seated satisfaction with each other from occurring. It takes a combination of the power of God, of time and a little fire for this to occur.

That one way you discover who you are is by Spirit-encounters in the word, like Jesus and Paul experienced? Yes, this is the pattern God has laid out in the life of Abraham who is the father of faith and the father of the out-working of faith which is righteousness. A significant part of righteousness is becoming and knowing the you God imagined—the one who is right with God and with himself. As your father, Abraham's life is the pattern for your life as well.

God spoke only a few things to Abraham about his life, but He said them over and over. The Lord then arranged various experiences through which these words could come to pass. God took him through the faith, hope and love process.

I have found that this process has been worked out in my life as well. God has used a few specific words to grow me into my destiny as I have held on to them when there was no reason to, other than God said it. Your destiny is hidden in the Word for you to discover, as well.

That praying spirit-words (praying in tongues) is a Christian thing and not just a charismatic thing? I do not presently attend a charismatic church, and yet I pray daily, and often, with spirit-words. And I can honestly say that praying this way has always been matter of fact. I have never had goose bumps, visions of God

AFTERWORD

or heard audible voices. But I have experienced what Paul said I would. In 1 Corinthians 14, he said five things about praying from the spirit–why it is important and why it is largely for private use.

1) My audience would be God. It certainly is not people. I have sensed His presence at times when I have connected with Him this way from my spirit. 2) I speak mysteries. Mysteries are things that God has hidden but wants to reveal to your understanding. I am convinced that even some of this writing is a direct result of my praying from my spirit. From the pool of my spirit-words, the Holy Spirit took His thimble, dipped it into His vast knowledge and poured a little bit into my heart. The Christian faith is a revelatory faith, and, I believe, praying this way invites revelation. 3) Praying spirit-words is equivalent to charging your battery. That is what Paul said. When you pray in the spirit, you edify yourself. If God has given you a way to build yourself up, why not use it? I don't think you can effectively build anyone else up anyway, unless you are edifying yourself. (There are other ways to do edify yourself obviously, but Paul says specifically that praying from your spirit does.) 4) When you pray in tongues, your spirit prays. I can't emphasize how important this is. The church is largely unaware how vast that space is. Your spirit is where the Triune dwells. It is the Holy of Holies and God has given you a way to release and express what is happening there. 5) You give thanks well. Your worship is heightened and expanded and deepened while you commune and communicate from your spirit.

Paul said praying is not either/or but both/and. He prayed to the extent of his understanding and then prayed beyond that with his spirit. The church has made the "baptism in the Holy Spirit" either a non-event or a special event with some particular formulas. The only formula is this: Jesus has already proven to be Lord via His ascension and, as a result, has poured out upon all flesh, His Spirit. For the nonbeliever, this means that a little crack of honesty toward God is all that it takes for regeneration. The Spirit rushes in to bring salvation.

For those who have received Christ, another gift is offered. In John 14, Jesus told His disciples that the Spirit was with them but would be in them. Then in John 20, He breathed on them and told them to receive the Spirit. New birth occurred.

AFTERWORD

In Luke, however, the disciples were told to wait until the Spirit came on them. In Luke's 2nd book, we see the Spirit coming on them with accompanying signs. In and on. These are the two aspects of the Spirit in the life of the believer—experiencing Jesus as the Lamb slain for forgiveness and as the Lion filling you with His roar. Tongues is one way to release that roar.

Part of what happened at Pentecost was God capturing the disciple's tongue. James said that no man can tame his own tongue. So why not let the Spirit? While I don't believe that you have less of the Spirit if this has not been your experience, I do say, if this offered to all of His children, why not avail yourself to receive Him in this way? If you are one of his children, you already have permission to pray this way. So what is stopping you?

As I mentioned, praying from the spirit is as matter of fact as praying with your understanding. Since you already can express your mind and heart through your mouth, you can also express the spirit's thoughts through your mouth as well. At least that has been my experience and what I have seen in Scriptures. Praying spirit-words will add dimensions to your life that you can never have imagined.

About warfare being largely about keeping yourself in the love of God? Yes to that as well. The church needs to do a better job of clarifying this and teaching the saints how to live in an awareness of His great multi-layered love.

Before I close, let me address one last thing—the title. It includes "a Transliteration." As I sent this out to various people to read, I got some push back on that because this book seems a whole lot more like a paraphrase.

Touché. It is paraphrase in the literal sense of the word. A transliteration is different than translating. With a translation, one finds a corresponding word in your language that approximates the word in the other. A paraphrase embellishes on the word or thought and paints pictures that might help get the meaning across.

A transliteration realizes that there are no words in your language that convey the meaning of word you are trying to translate. So you must create a new word and then apply meaning to it. In the English Bible, the words apostle and angel were made up words.

AFTERWORD

There is no word in our internal language that approximates words like God, grace, righteousness and the like. I was once in a meeting where the leader said, "We all knows what grace means." I said, "I have no clue." And I still don't, though I think I am looking in the right direction.

Yes, these words have a definition, but they have no meaning to us. There needs to be a new word found in your own personal language that creates an "aha" moment, and a growing understanding. To a large degree, this is subjective.

And really isn't this why Jesus became flesh? The written word needed to be transliterated so He became that new, created word by which we understand everything about life. Jesus is the transliteration of God.

This experiment for me was a transliteration. My internal language had no words for the love of God and I had no definition for myself. My writing this has helped process in me. Not sure, if this explanation has helped clarify why I had transliteration in the title, but there was a method to my madness.

I trust that this book has opened your heart a little more to the possibility of God. It has mine. This book for me has been a primer into more of God and that is my hope for you as well. I don't expect that you embrace everything I have written as gospel, but I hope that you would begin to see God in a different way.

God is outside of your theology and, if you have opened your heart to him, is inside of your darkness. He is both God most High and God most nigh. He is the unapproachable Approachable. Like David, I hope you hear His "yes" though others might be telling you "no."

And as you reread and consider thoughts written in this book, I pray that you discover the God you could never have imagined, and the you God imagined before the worlds began.

www.ingramcontent.com/pod-product-compliance
Lightning Source LLC
Chambersburg PA
CBHW070923160426
43193CB00011B/1563